Collins

11+
Maths

Complete Revision, Practice & Assessment

For GL Assessment

Introduction

The 11+ Maths Test

In most cases, the 11+ selection tests are set by GL Assessment, CEM or the individual school. You should be able to find out which tests your child will be taking on the website of the school they are applying to or from the local authority.

Mathematics tests are used by schools to assess the ability of each child and determine whether they have attained the required standard of mathematical skills, reasoning and problem-solving.

It is particularly important to provide maths practice as the 11+ tests may test skills that are slightly more advanced than those on the national curriculum for your child's age.

About this Book

This book is split into three sections to help your child to prepare for the GL Assessment test in mathematics. Features of each section include:

Revision
- Easy-to-digest revision notes for each topic.
- Develops the skills needed to answer test questions.
- 'Remember' boxes to emphasise key points and provide tips.
- Quick Tests to check understanding before moving on.

Practice
- Topic-based questions to practise the necessary skills.
- Increases familiarity with the questions expected in the test.
- Tests are timed to develop working at speed.

Assessment
- Four practice papers offer multiple opportunities to have a go at a test and gradually improve performance.
- Familiarises your child with the format of the papers.
- Enables your child to practise working at speed and with accuracy.

Answers and explanations are provided at the back of the book to help you mark your child's answers and support their preparation.

Progress charts are also included to help you record scores on the practice tests and practice papers.

ebook

To access the ebook visit collins.co.uk/ebooks and follow the step-by-step instructions.

The Practice Papers

Spend some time talking with your child so that they understand the purpose of the practice papers and how doing them will help them to prepare for the actual exam.

Agree with your child a good time to take the practice papers. This should be when they are fresh and alert. You also need to find a good place to work, a place that is comfortable and free from distractions. Being able to see a clock is helpful as they learn how to pace themselves.

Explain how they may find some parts easy and others more challenging, but that they need to have a go at every question. If they 'get stuck' on a question, they should just mark it with an asterisk and carry on. At the end of the paper, they may have time to go back and try again.

Multiple-choice tests

For this style of test, the answers are recorded on a separate answer sheet and not in the question booklet. This answer sheet will often be marked by a computer for the actual exam, so it is important that it is used correctly.

Answers should be indicated by drawing a clear pencil line through the appropriate box and there should be no other marks. If your child indicates one answer and then wants to change their response, the first mark must be fully rubbed out. Practising with an answer sheet now will reduce the chance of your child getting anxious or confused during the actual test.

The answer sheets for the practice papers can be found at the very back of the book on pages 161–168. Further copies of these answer sheets can be downloaded from **collins.co.uk/11plus**.

How much time should be given?

Allowing 50 minutes for each of these practice papers will give your child experience of the most likely test format. If your child has not finished after 50 minutes, ask them to draw a line to indicate where they are on the paper at that time, and allow them to finish. This allows them to practise every question type, as well as allowing you to get a score showing how many were correctly answered in the time available. It will also help you and your child to think about ways to increase speed of working if this is an area that your child finds difficult.

If your child completes the paper in less than 50 minutes, encourage them to go through and check their answers carefully.

Marking

Award one mark for each correct answer. Half marks are not allowed. No marks are deducted for wrong answers.

If scores are low, look at the paper and identify which question types seem to be harder for your child. Then spend some time going over them together. If your child is very accurate and gets correct answers, but works too slowly, try getting them to do one of the practice papers with time targets going through. If you are helpful and look for ways to help your child, they will grow in confidence and feel well prepared when they take the actual exam.

Note: The practice papers are designed to reflect the style of GL Assessment tests, but the score achieved on these papers is no guarantee that your child will achieve a score of the same standard on the formal tests. Other factors, such as the standard of responses from all pupils who took the test, will determine their success in the formal exam.

Acknowledgements

All images are © Shutterstock.com or
© HarperCollinsPublishers Ltd 2020

Every effort has been made to trace copyright holders and obtain their permission for the use of copyright material. The authors and publisher will gladly receive information enabling them to rectify any error or omission in subsequent editions. All facts are correct at time of going to press.

Published by Collins
An imprint of HarperCollinsPublishers
1 London Bridge Street
London SE1 9GF

HarperCollinsPublishers
Macken House
39/40 Mayor Street Upper
Dublin 1
D01 C9W8
Ireland

ISBN: 978-0-00-839885-9

First published 2020

10 9 8 7 6 5

© HarperCollinsPublishers Ltd 2020

British Library Cataloguing in Publication Data.

A CIP record of this book is available from the British Library.

Publishers: Clare Souza and Katie Sergeant
Contributing authors: Leisa Bovey, Val Mitchell, Sally Moon, Donna Hanley and Rosie Benton
Project Development and Management: Richard Toms and Rebecca Skinner
Reviewers: Maravandio Ltd (trading as The Sensible Tuition Company) and Deborah Dobson
Cover Design: Kevin Robbins and Sarah Duxbury
Inside Concept Design: Ian Wrigley
Page Layout: Jouve India Private Limited
Production: Karen Nulty
Printed in the United Kingdom

This book contains FSC™ certified paper and other controlled sources to ensure responsible forest management.

For more information visit: www.harpercollins.co.uk/green

Contents

Revision

Number and Place Value 6
Calculations 10
Fractions, Decimals and Percentages 18
Ratio and Proportion 26
Algebra 29
Measurement 35
Geometry 44
Statistics 51

Practice

Practice Test 1: Number and Place Value 58
Practice Test 2: Calculations 60
Practice Test 3: Fractions, Decimals and Percentages 64
Practice Test 4: Ratio and Proportion 68
Practice Test 5: Algebra 72
Practice Test 6: Measurement 76
Practice Test 7: Geometry 82
Practice Test 8: Statistics 88

Assessment

Practice Paper 1 95
Practice Paper 2 107
Practice Paper 3 121
Practice Paper 4 137

Answers

Revision Answers 150
Practice Answers 152
Assessment Answers 155

Progress Charts 160
Practice Paper Answer Sheets 161

Number and Place Value

You should be able to:

- read, write and interpret numbers expressed as numerals and in words
- order positive and negative numbers
- round a number to the nearest ten, hundred or thousand
- solve problems using numerical reasoning.

Place Value and Reading and Writing Numbers

- Place value means that with only 10 digits (0, 1, 2, 3, 4, 5, 6, 7, 8, 9) you can write any number of any size.
- The table shows some positions and their place values:

9	6	5	3	8	1	4	.	7	2
MILLIONS	HUNDRED THOUSANDS	TEN THOUSANDS	THOUSANDS	HUNDREDS	TENS	ONES (UNITS)	DECIMAL POINT	TENTHS	HUNDREDTHS

> **Remember**
>
> The position of each digit in a number is related to its magnitude (i.e. its size).

- If asked how many thousands there are in a number, look at the thousands column and read the numeral in that position. In the number 9 653 814.72 there are three thousands.

Example

How many hundreds are there in the number 27 978?

27 978

There are **9** hundreds.

- To read, write and talk about these numbers they get grouped together like this:
- The number 9 653 814.72 written as words is: nine million, six hundred and fifty-three thousand, eight hundred and point seven two.

9	6	5 3	8	1 4	.	7	2
Million	Hundred and	Thousand	Hundred and		Point		

> **Remember**
>
> Be careful when there are places that contain zeros. The number three thousand and ninety-two has no hundreds; it is the same as 'three thousand, no hundreds and ninety-two'. In numerals that is 3092.

Example

What is 403 055 in words?

Four hundred and three thousand and fifty-five

Ordering Whole Numbers

- Ordering numbers is about place value. Check whether you are ordering largest to smallest, or smallest to largest.
- Write the numbers in columns containing thousands, hundreds, tens and ones.

Example

Order these numbers from smallest to largest:

91, 996, 936, 6, 1, 19, 29, 0, 9360, 963

For ordering whole numbers, group the numbers depending on how many digits they have, then order them within each column:

6	91	996	9360
1	29	963	
0	19	936	

The correct order of the numbers, smallest to largest, is:

0 1 6 19 29 91 936 963 996 9360

> **Remember**
>
> When ordering negative numbers, the process is reversed, i.e. two-digit numbers are smaller than one-digit numbers. For example, −60 is less than −5.

Number Lines

- Number lines help you to think about the relative positions of numbers.
- Some number lines include negative numbers. The numbers become more negative as they move left (or down). You may need to interpret these numbers in a given context.
- When reading a number line:
  - make sure you check what the labelled numbers go up in
  - look at how the gaps between the numbers are divided up and check the sub-divisions make sense.

> **Remember**
>
> Examples of number lines used in real life are the measurements along the edge of a ruler or the scale on a thermometer.

Example

Read the points labelled A, B and C on the number line below.

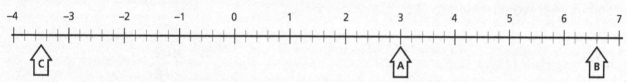

The point A is at a labelled point so can be read straight off. **A = 3**

The point B is on one of the sub-divisions. The gap between labelled points is 1. There are five steps (sub-divisions) between each labelled point so the smaller divisions are steps of 1 ÷ 5 = 0.2. You can check this by writing in the steps.

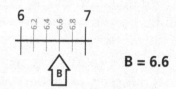

B = 6.6

The point C sits in the middle of two sub-divisions. What number is halfway between −3.4 and −3.6?

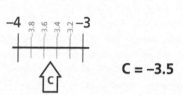

C = −3.5

- You can use number lines to count on or back from a given number too.

Example

This is a picture of the thermometer in Sarah's greenhouse.

The greenhouse is 7.5°C warmer than outside.

What is the temperature outside?

Each small sub-division is 2.5°C.

So the reading on this thermometer is –2.5°C.

7.5°C colder would be **–10°C**.

Rounding Whole Numbers

- Not all rounding questions use the word 'rounding'. Other words used include 'sensible', and 'roughly'.
- Before you begin, check which place value you are rounding to: tens, hundreds or thousands.
- When rounding to tens, look at the digit in the ones (units) column: digits 1 to 4 round to the ten below; digits 5 to 9 round to the ten above.

All round down to 20 to the nearest ten.

All round up to 30 to the nearest ten.

◄——————————————————————►

20 21 22 23 24 25 26 27 28 29 30

- When rounding to hundreds, look at the digit in the tens column and apply the same rule. So, for example, all numbers from 150 to 249 would round to 200 to the nearest hundred.
- When rounding to thousands, look at the digit in the hundreds column and apply the same rule. So, for example, all numbers from 2500 to 3499 would round to 3000 to the nearest thousand.

Problem Solving with Numbers

- Using your number knowledge, it is possible to solve questions in unfamiliar contexts.
- To find a number halfway between two given numbers:
  - Add the two numbers together and divide by 2; this is quick but the calculation might be complicated.
  - Count, on a number line, back from one number and forward from the other until you meet in the middle – keep careful track of doing the same from both sides as it can be easy to forget and move further from one side than the other.

> **Remember**
>
> If a number is exactly halfway between two tens, two hundreds or two thousands, the rule is **round up**.

> **Remember**
>
> There are often lots of ways to come up with solutions to mathematical questions. Use the way that makes sense to you and think about how you could explain your method to someone else.

- Find how big the gap is between the two numbers (take the smaller one away from the larger), halve the answer, then add it onto the smaller number (or take it away from the larger number).

Example

What number is halfway between 17 and 35?

$17 + 35 = 52$ $\frac{52}{2} = 26$	~~17~~, ~~18~~, ~~19~~, ~~20~~, ~~21~~, ~~22~~, ~~23~~, ~~24~~, 25, ~~26~~, ~~27~~, ~~28~~, ~~29~~, ~~30~~, ~~31~~, ~~32~~, ~~33~~, ~~34~~, ~~35~~ <small>Ensure that an equal number of values are crossed out on each side.</small>	$35 - 17 = 18$ $\frac{18}{2} = 9$ $17 + 9 = 26$

- For problem-solving questions, often the best approach is to try something, test it out and see if it helps to find a way towards a solution. If a method is taking a long time, then look for any patterns or shortcuts that you could use.

Example

Arenya is playing a game where she spins a spinner to get a starting number. She then counts up by 3, then 7, then 3, then 7, and so on. She wins the game if she gets to say the number 37. Which number(s) on the spinner must Arenya get on the spinner in order to win?

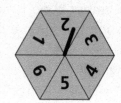

Since 3 and 7 are number bonds to 10 (i.e. $3 + 7 = 10$), the units as she counts will repeat so it is possible to see whether a starting point will give a result of 37 without needing to do the counting beyond 37 for each number.

Starting at 1, 4, 11, 14, ... this will not give 37 as it will always have a final digit of 1 or 4.

2, 5, 12, 15, ... 3, 6, 13, 16, ...

4, 7, 14, 17, ... starting on 4 will get to 37.

5, 8, 15, 18, ... 6, 9, 16, 19, ...

4 is the only number that will get her to 37.

> **Quick Test**
>
> 1. Write the number ten thousand and sixty-five in numerals.
> 2. Write the number 370 806 in words.
> 3. The price of a house is £224 945. What is this rounded to:
>   a) the nearest ten?   b) the nearest thousand?
>   c) the nearest hundred thousand?
> 4. Which of these cities is the coldest?
>   A Birmingham 0°C   B Exeter 8°C   C Leeds −3°C
>   D London 5°C   E Newcastle −8°C
> 5. These six-digit numbers are listed in order but some of the digits have been replaced by boxes. Fill in the missing digits.
>   342 95☐
>   342 ☐51
>   ☐49 808
>   3☐9 806
>   359 ☐45

Calculations

You should be able to:

- find an efficient method to add, subtract, multiply and divide numbers
- solve complex multiplications and divisions
- choose the correct operation to solve and follow the BIDMAS rule
- use rounding to predict answers and check for accuracy.

Mental Strategies

Addition and Subtraction Shortcuts

- Although you can always use the column method for additions and subtractions, many questions can be solved by using number bond facts you already know.
- Look for number bonds within lists to speed up addition.

Example
To add up this list, first identify pairs that you can add easily, then complete the final addition:

109	4	1	91	15

$109 + 91 = 200$ $4 + 1 = 5$, then $5 + 15 = 20$
$200 + 20 = \mathbf{220}$

- When subtracting, move the 'gap' between numbers to speed up the calculation. Add an equal value to each number to simplify the calculation. Here the value added is 2:
$98 - 72 = \longrightarrow 100 - 74 =$
- To add or subtract a number, round the 'almost multiple' up or down, calculate and adjust.

Example
$307 + 199 = ?$

$307 + 200 = 507$ $507 - 1 = \mathbf{506}$

Example
$307 - 199 = ?$

$307 - 200 = 107$ $107 + 1 = \mathbf{108}$

- When working with positive and negative numbers, it helps to visualise a number line. Moving from left to right along the number line shown here represents addition; working from right to left indicates subtraction.

 Remember

Moving the 'gap' is a method that only works with subtraction.

 Remember

Subtracting a negative number means that you add it. For example:
$3 - (-7) = 10$

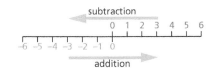

Example

−3 + 4 = ?

Begin at −3 on the number line. Move four numbers to the right to find the answer.

−3 + 4 = **+1**

Example

−3 − 2 = ?

Begin at −3 on the number line. Move two numbers to the left to find the answer.

−3 − 2 = **−5**

- When carrying out calculations, you can use partitioning to break down numbers into easier-to-use values, for example thinking of 837 as 800 + 30 + 7.

Example

536 + 628 = ?

Partition both numbers:

536	=	500	+	30	+	6		
628	=	600	+	20	+	8		
Total	=	1100	+	50	+	14	=	**1164**

Multiplication and Division Shortcuts

- Many multiplication and division questions can be solved by using already-known number bond facts.
- Use multiplication tables that you know and look for ways to partition numbers.

Example

17 × 5 = ?

17 × 5 can be split into: 10 × 5 = 50   7 × 5 = 35

Then add the numbers back together:

$$17 \times 5 \begin{cases} 10 \times 5 = 50 \\ 7 \times 5 = 35 \end{cases} = \textbf{85}$$

- To multiply and divide by 10, 100 and 1000: move digits to the left when multiplying, and to the right when dividing.
- When dividing, you may have to cross the decimal point.

Example

25 × 10 = 250   25 ÷ 100 = 0.25

25 × 100 = 2500   250 ÷ 10 = 25

25 × 1000 = 25 000   2500 ÷ 100 = 25

- When multiplying by the numbers 9, 99 and 999:
  Round the 9, 99 or 999 to 10, 100 or 1000 and adjust by subtraction.

Remember

Use inverse operations to check that your answer is correct.

For example, 2456 + 172 = 2628, so that means 2628 − 172 = 2456.

Remember

There are lots of different ways to approach addition and subtraction, which means there is always a way to double check an answer by using a second method.

Example

56 × 9 = ?

56 × 9 = (56 × 10) − 56
56 × 10 = 560   560 − 56 = **504**

- Your knowledge of doubling and halving numbers can also help solve some problems.
- To multiply by 4, double the number twice.

Example

22 × 4 = ?

22 × 2 = 44   and   44 × 2 = **88**

- To divide by 4, halve the number twice.

Example

248 ÷ 4 = ?

248 ÷ 2 = 124   and   124 ÷ 2 = **62**

Formal Written Methods

Multiplication

- There are two common methods for solving multiplications:

Column method

```
      3 6 2
×       4 3
  1 0,8 6   (362 × 3)
1 4,4 8 0   (362 × 40)
1 5 5,6 6
```

Grid method

×	300	60	2
40	12000	2400	80
3	900	180	6

          12900   2580   86
12900 + 2580 + 86 = 15566

You must partition the numbers correctly, e.g. 362 = 300 + 60 + 2

Division

- Use a formal method to solve more complex division questions:

```
    1 2 3 0
8 9 ¹8 ²4 0
```

- Sometimes a number will divide exactly, leaving a whole number answer; sometimes a division calculation will leave a remainder.
- Division calculations can be thought of as sharing. If you imagine sharing a bag of 19 marbles between a group of five friends, each time round everyone is given a marble. After three rounds, everyone has three marbles but now there are only four marbles left. These four marbles can't be shared fairly between the five friends. The four marbles are the remainder (what is left over when everything that could be divided up in whole parts has been).
- Sometimes it is more appropriate to round the remainder up or down.

> **Remember**
>
> Clue words can suggest the question is about multiplication or division.
>
> Common words for multiplication are: 'altogether', 'total', 'product', 'times' and 'lots of'.
>
> Clue words for division include: 'share', 'remainder', 'left over' and 'quotient'.

Example

Charlie has 57 marbles and wants to share them evenly between his eight friends. How many marbles will each person get and will there be any left over?

$57 \div 8$

$56 = 7 \times 8$, $57 - 56 = 1$

$$57 \div 8 = 7 \text{ remainder } 1$$

Each person will get **7 marbles** and there will be **1 left over**.

Example

A school has 353 students in a year group. The students must be split into classes of 30. How many classes will there be in this year group?

$353 \div 30$

$300 \div 30 = 10$, $30 \div 30 = 1$,

$330 \div 30 = 11$

$353 \div 30 = 11$ remainder 23

There would need to be **12 classes** as there are more than 330 students (which would be 11 classes) and the 23 remaining students need to be included in a class.

Carrying Out the Correct Operations

- Some questions will involve more than one operation and you will need to identify what these are.

Example

Anwar had 385 CDs. He put them into boxes that held 30 each. How many full boxes did he have?

The question could be solved by repeated subtraction or simple division.

$385 - (10 \times 30) = 85$ and $85 - (2 \times 30) = 25$

So there are **12 full boxes** (with 25 CDs left over).

BIDMAS

- BIDMAS is an easy way to remember the order in which operations should be completed:
  Brackets first... then **I**ndices (powers), then **D**ivision and **M**ultiplication, then **A**ddition and **S**ubtraction
- When there are brackets, you must do the calculation within the brackets first otherwise the answer may be incorrect. So $(6 + 3) \times 3 = 27$.
- Without the brackets, the multiplication must be done first, so $6 + 3 \times 3 = 15$.

> **Remember**
>
> Use inverse operations to check that your answer is correct. For example, $17 \times 5 = 85$, so that means $85 \div 5 = 17$.

> **Remember**
>
> The order in which you perform a calculation can affect the answer.

Estimating and Checking

- Rounding helps you to roughly predict an answer or to check if a calculation is sensible.

Example

$2367 + 3945 + 4210 = ?$

Rounding to the nearest thousand, this becomes:

$2000 + 4000 + 4000 =$

The answer should be roughly 10 000.

- When you are estimating answers involving large numbers, look for numbers that can be rounded up or down.

Example

$24 \times 693 + 76 \times 591 = ?$

A 6200 **B** 61 548 **C** 69 540 **D** 32 560 **E** 58 623 241

The numbers can be rounded to: $20 \times 700 + 80 \times 600 =$

Remembering BIDMAS, $14\,000 + 48\,000 = 62\,000$

Choose the answer closest to the estimate; the answer is **B**.

Remember

If the question involves making something smaller, this indicates subtraction or division.

If the question involves making something bigger, this indicates addition or multiplication.

Factors and Multiples

- **Factors** are all the values that a number can be **divided** by exactly without leaving a remainder. Factors occur in pairs.

Example

To work out the factors of 12: 1×12 2×6 3×4

So the factors of 12 are: 1, 2, 3, 4, 6 and 12

- When finding the factors of a square number, one pair will be the same value multiplied by itself.

Example

To work out the factors of 16: 1×16 2×8 (4×4)

You only write each factor once: 1, 2, 4, 8, 16

- **Prime numbers** only have two factors: 1 and the number itself.

Remember

Numbers that are not prime and are greater than 1 are called **composite numbers**.

- **Multiples** of a number are what you get when you multiply that number by different whole numbers, so the answers are in the multiplication (times) table for that number.

Example

The first six multiples of 5 are: 5   10   15   20   25   30
The first six multiples of 22 are: 22   44   66   88   110   132

- Problems involving factors or multiples can be presented in real-life situations, however the calculation is just the same.

Example

A number 11 bus arrives at the depot every 20 minutes. A number 6 bus arrives at the depot every 50 minutes. If they both arrive at the depot at 9 am, at what time will they next arrive together?

The easiest way to tackle this question is to write out the multiples as a multiplication table. You are working in minutes, so remember that 60 minutes make an hour.

Bus number 11: 09.00   09.20   09.40   10.00   10.20   (10.40)
Bus number 6:   09.00   09.50   (10.40)

The answer is **10.40**

Finding Common Multiples and Factors

- Different numbers can have factors that are the same. These are called 'common factors'.
- The highest common factor (HCF) is the highest number that divides exactly into all the numbers listed.

Example

What is the HCF of these four numbers? 24   36   48   60
The HCF is **12**.

- Different multiplication tables can also have numbers in common. These are called 'common multiples'.

Example

What is the least common multiple (LCM) of 3 and 4?

Multiples of 3: 3, 6, 9, (12), 15, 18, 21, (24), 27, 30, 33, (36), etc.
Multiples of 4: 4, 8, (12), 16, 20, (24), 28, 32, (36), etc.

The common multiples of 3 and 4 are: 12, 24, 36, etc.
The least (i.e. the lowest) common multiple is therefore **12**.

Square and Cube Numbers

- Square numbers are found by multiplying a number by itself (also known as squaring it).
- They are called square numbers because each of the numbers could be represented by dots in a square pattern (see right).

- The square numbers form a sequence. Looking at the diagram to the right, the next square number can be found by squaring 5 (5 × 5 = 25) or it can be found by adding 9 to the previous square number (16 + 9 = 25).
- Cube numbers can be represented by a sequence of cubes. As shown, the cube numbers can be calculated by cubing a number, i.e. multiplying the same number by itself twice.

$1 \times 1 \times 1 = 1$

$2 \times 2 \times 2 = 8$

$3 \times 3 \times 3 = 27$

$4 \times 4 \times 4 = 64$

Problem Solving

- **Number machines** are a set of instructions that show the steps in a calculation that change the input number (the one you start with) into the output (the number at the end). Using inverse operations enables you to operate the number machine 'in reverse'.

Example

Jessica sets up a number machine as shown below.

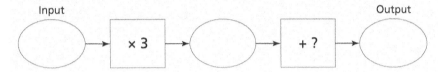

When she inputs 1, the answer is 29. What would the input number be if Jessica's machine gave an output of 50?

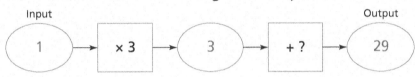

If 1 is input, the middle value is 3. 29 − 3 = 26 so the number machine adds 26.

Now use the inverse operations through the machine to find the answer.

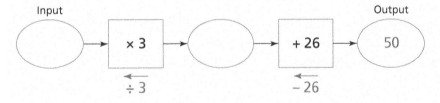

50 − 26 = 24   24 ÷ 3 = 8

The input was **8**.

> **Remember**
>
> Problem solving generally involves looking at a problem that is unfamiliar and applying the relevant skills to work out a solution.

- You might be presented with an incomplete grid, for example three squares wide by three squares long, where each row and each column must add up to the same value.

Example

This magic square has some empty spaces. When every space is filled in, each row and each column adds up to 27.
What number should be in the space with the question mark?

8		10	→ 27
12	?		→ 27
		7	→ 27

↓ 27   ↓ 27   ↓ 27

Start with the rows or columns that have just one missing number:
The top row: 8 + ☐ + 10 = 27, so the missing number in the top row must be 9.
The first column: 8 + 12 + ☐ = 27, so the missing number in the bottom left square is 7.
Now the remaining empty space in the bottom row can be filled:
7 + ☐ + 7 = 27, so the missing number in the bottom row of the second column must be 13.
So the missing number in the space marked ? is: 9 + ☐ + 13 = 27, giving an answer of **5**.
The fully-completed square is shown right.

8	9	10	→ 27
12	5	10	→ 27
7	13	7	→ 27

↓ 27   ↓ 27   ↓ 27

- You may need to work out a problem to find a mystery number.

Example

Hassan is thinking of a number. He divides his number by 25 and the answer is a whole number. Which of these could be his number?

A 710   **B** 715   **C** 720   **D** 725   **E** 730

If Hassan's answer is a whole number, the number he has thought of must be a multiple of 25:

$25 \times 1 = 25$, $25 \times 2 = 50$, $25 \times 3 = 75$, $25 \times 4 = 100$,
$25 \times 5 = 125$, $25 \times 6 = 150$, $25 \times 7 = 175$, $25 \times 8 = 200$, etc.

We can see that each multiple ends in the digits 25, 50, 75 or 00. Only one of the options, **725**, fits into this pattern of digits so the answer is **D**.

> **Remember**
>
> Always think about what you know and use your mathematical toolbox to help you fill in the gaps to solve the problem.

Quick Test

1. Which of these lists contains only multiples of 4 or 5?
   A 12, 14, 15   B 8, 12, 13   C 8, 9, 10   D 8, 10, 11   E 12, 15, 16
2. How many factors of 36 are also square numbers?
3. One lighthouse flashes every 45 seconds. Another flashes every 50 seconds. If they flash together at exactly 9 pm, how many seconds will pass before they flash together again?
4. A magic square is shown in which each row and each column sums to the same total. It contains the even numbers from 4 to 20. Complete the square.

10		
	8	16
		14

5. I am thinking of a number. I multiply it by 6 and add 3 to the answer. I then subtract 8 and the final answer is 55. What was my original number?

Fractions, Decimals and Percentages

You should be able to:

- calculate with fractions, decimals and percentages
- find equivalent fractions, decimals and percentages
- calculate probabilities using fractions, decimals and percentages.

Comparing and Ordering Fractions

- To generate equivalent fractions, write out the fraction then multiply the numerator and the denominator by the same value.

Example

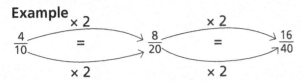

>
> **Remember**
>
> The top digit in a fraction is called the numerator and the bottom digit is called the denominator.

- To find a fraction in its lowest terms, divide the numerator and the denominator by the highest common factor (HCF).

Example

Express $\frac{16}{40}$ in its lowest terms.

The HCF of the numerator and the denominator is 8.

$16 \div 8 = 2$ $\qquad$ $40 \div 8 = 5$

$\frac{2}{5}$ is the fraction in its lowest terms.

- To write a set of fractions in order quickly, adjust the fractions so that the denominators are all the same value:
  - The common denominator will be a common multiple.
  - For simplicity, work with the lowest common multiple.

Example

Order these fractions, starting with the smallest:

$\frac{1}{2}$ $\qquad$ $\frac{5}{6}$ $\qquad$ $\frac{3}{4}$ $\qquad$ $\frac{7}{12}$ $\qquad$ $\frac{2}{3}$

Find the lowest common multiple. This is 12. Change all the fractions to twelfths (whichever number you multiply the denominator by to get 12, you do the same for the numerator):

$\frac{6}{12}$ $\qquad$ $\frac{10}{12}$ $\qquad$ $\frac{9}{12}$ $\qquad$ $\frac{7}{12}$ $\qquad$ $\frac{8}{12}$

Now order the fractions by the numerators, starting with the smallest:

$\frac{6}{12}$ $\qquad$ $\frac{7}{12}$ $\qquad$ $\frac{8}{12}$ $\qquad$ $\frac{9}{12}$ $\qquad$ $\frac{10}{12}$

In the original format: $\frac{1}{2}$ $\frac{7}{12}$ $\frac{2}{3}$ $\frac{3}{4}$ $\frac{5}{6}$

> **Remember**
>
> Improper fractions have a numerator equal to or greater than the denominator. They are equivalent to a whole or a mixed number.

- To simplify or write an improper fraction as a mixed number, it is useful to know your times tables to identify multiples quickly. You first need to find the whole number.

Example

What is $\frac{74}{8}$ as a mixed number in its lowest terms?

To write this number in its lowest terms, see how many times 8 fits into 74: $8 \times 9 = 72$

This makes 9 the whole number and the fraction left is $\frac{2}{8}$, which can then be simplified to $\frac{1}{4}$.

So $\frac{74}{8} = 9\frac{1}{4}$

Adding and Subtracting Fractions

- The process for adding and subtracting fractions begins in the same way as for ordering fractions – change the denominators to a common number. Once the denominators are the same, you can then add or subtract the numerators.

Remember

Don't add or subtract the denominators.

Example

$$\frac{2}{3} - \frac{1}{6} \quad = \quad \frac{4}{6} - \frac{1}{6} \quad = \quad \frac{3}{6}$$

Simplify the fraction to its lowest terms to find the answer.

$$\frac{3}{6} = \frac{1}{2}$$

Multiplying and Dividing Fractions

- The first step in multiplying and dividing fractions is to make sure they are not written as mixed numbers.
- To multiply, write as a single fraction where the numerators are multiplied by each other and the denominators are multiplied by each other. Before doing the multiplications, you can look for common factors and simplify if possible.

Remember

Always check if the final answer can be simplified any further.

Example

$$\frac{2}{3} \times \frac{5}{6} \quad = \quad \frac{2 \times 5}{3 \times 6} \quad = \quad \frac{1 \times 5}{3 \times 3} \quad = \quad \frac{5}{9}$$

- To divide, use the fact that multiplication and division are inverse operations. For example, multiplying by $\frac{1}{4}$ is the same as dividing by 4, so dividing by $\frac{1}{4}$ is the same as multiplying by 4.
- Dividing by a fraction is the same as multiplying by its inverse. For example, dividing by $\frac{5}{7}$ is the same as multiplying by $\frac{7}{5}$.
- Convert any mixed numbers to improper fractions before you carry out the operation.

Example

$$1\frac{3}{5} \div 1\frac{1}{15} \quad = \quad \frac{8}{5} \div \frac{16}{15} \quad = \quad \frac{8}{5} \times \frac{15}{16}$$

$$= \quad \frac{8 \times 15}{5 \times 16} \quad = \quad \frac{1 \times 3}{1 \times 2}$$

$$= \quad \frac{3}{2} \quad = \quad 1\frac{1}{2}$$

Calculating Fractions of an Amount

- Use division to find a simple fraction of a given amount.
  So, to find $\frac{1}{3}$ of £27, divide £27 by the denominator 3.
- To find a fraction with a numerator greater than 1, you also need to multiply. To find $\frac{2}{3}$ of £27, divide £27 by 3 and multiply by the numerator 2.
- To find out the total amount from a fraction, both division and multiplication are needed again.

Example

If 30 grams is $\frac{3}{5}$ the weight of a box of pencils, what is the total weight of the box?

You need to find out what one part ($\frac{1}{5}$) of the amount equals first.
So divide 30 grams by the numerator to find the value of $\frac{1}{5}$, then multiply by the denominator to find the total weight.

$30g \div 3 = 10g \qquad 10g \times 5 = \mathbf{50g}$

- When you calculate fractions of real-life things, a diagram can help.

Example

If five pizzas are shared between six children, what fraction of a pizza does each child get?

Begin by working out how much of a single pizza each child would receive. To do this you need to divide one pizza into six, i.e. one piece for each child.

You now know that a child will have $\frac{1}{6}$ of a single pizza, so this makes it easier to calculate the fraction they would receive from five pizzas.

$\frac{1}{6} \times 5 = \frac{5}{6}$, so each child will receive $\frac{5}{6}$ of a pizza.

- Some probability questions are fraction questions in disguise.

Example

What is the probability of throwing an even number on a regular, six-sided dice?
There are six possible numbers. The denominator is 6.

1   2   3   4   5   6

There are three even numbers so the numerator is 3.
Therefore the probability is $\frac{3}{6}$ or $\frac{1}{2}$.

Quick Test

1. Put these fractions in order of size from smallest to largest: $\frac{11}{20}$ $\frac{4}{5}$ $\frac{1}{2}$ $\frac{3}{4}$ $\frac{7}{10}$
2. Which pair of these fractions add up to one whole? $\frac{5}{8}$ $\frac{2}{8}$ $\frac{1}{2}$ $\frac{3}{4}$ $\frac{7}{8}$
3. Write $4\frac{3}{8}$ as an improper fraction.
4. What fraction of the numbers in this list are **prime**? 1, 3, 5, 7, 9, 11, 13, 15, 17
5. Sunita spent £56 on some new trainers. After this she had $\frac{3}{10}$ of her money left. How much money does she have left?
6. Eric eats $\frac{2}{3}$ of a bag of sweets. Joanna eats $\frac{2}{3}$ of what is left, then Zoltan eats $\frac{2}{3}$ of what Joanna left. There are now 2 sweets in the bag. How many were there to start with?

Equivalent Fractions, Decimals and Percentages

- **Fractions** can also be written as a decimal or a percentage.
- **Decimals** can be written as fractions with a denominator that is a power of 10 (10, 100, 1000, etc.).
- To find a numerical fraction from a decimal, write it as a fraction, with the number of zeros to match the number of figures after the decimal point.

Example

$0.3 = \frac{3}{10}$ $0.03 = \frac{3}{100}$ $0.34 = \frac{34}{100}$

Check to see if the fractions can be simplified:

$0.3 = \frac{3}{10}$ $0.03 = \frac{3}{100}$ $0.34 = \frac{34}{100} = \frac{17}{50}$

- **Percentages** are fractions with a denominator of 100, such as:
  $1\% = \frac{1}{100}$ and $15\% = \frac{15}{100}$
- Percentages are not always whole numbers:
  $12.5\% = \frac{12.5}{100} = \frac{25}{200} = \frac{1}{8}$
- Percentages can be converted into decimals by dividing by 100 (move the digits two places to the right); so $12.5\% = 0.125$
- Learning the equivalents in the table by heart will help you work at speed.

> **Remember**
>
> The GL test is multiple choice and you can expect to have five answer options to choose from in each question.

Fraction	Decimal	Percentage
1	1.0	100%
$\frac{1}{2}$	0.5	50%
$\frac{1}{4}$	0.25	25%
$\frac{3}{4}$	0.75	75%
$\frac{1}{10}$	0.1	10%
$\frac{1}{5}$	0.2	20%
$\frac{1}{100}$	0.01	1%

- When you are asked to compare fractions with decimals or percentages, convert all the values to the same format to make them easier to compare.
- In the following example, converting all the values to decimals makes it easier to find the correct answer.

Example

Which of the following statements is correct?

A $2.25 = 2\frac{25}{10}$ **B** $2.25 = 2\frac{25}{50}$ **C** $2.25 = 2\frac{1}{4}$ **D** $2.25 = 2\frac{225}{100}$ **E** $2.25 = 22.5\%$

Change all the values to decimals:

A $2\frac{25}{10} = 2 + 2.5 = 4.5$ **B** $2\frac{25}{50} = 2 + \frac{50}{100} = 2.5$ **C** $2\frac{1}{4} = 2 + \frac{25}{100} = 2.25$

D $2\frac{225}{100} = 2 + 2 + \frac{25}{100} = 4.25$ **E** $22.5\% = 0.225$

Option **C** is the correct answer.

Comparing and Ordering Decimals

- Ordering decimals is an extension of ordering whole numbers (see page 7).
- To order a group of decimal numbers such as 1, 0.1, 0.01, 11.001, 1.023:
    - write the numbers in a vertical list, lining up the decimal point
    - fill in any gaps with zeros, as place holders, to avoid errors.
- Now the numbers can be easily ordered: 11.001, 1.023, 1, 0.1, 0.01

Calculations with Decimals

- When **adding** and **subtracting** decimals, line up the decimal points and insert any missing zeros as place holders, as shown right.
- Complete in the same way as a whole number addition or subtraction sum, remembering to keep the decimal point in the answer below the decimal point in the calculation.
- To **multiply** decimals, you can use your knowledge of division by 10s, or you can use estimation.

tens	ones (units)	decimal point	tenths	hundredths	thousandths
0	1	.	0	0	0
0	0	.	1	0	0
0	0	.	0	1	0
1	1	.	0	0	1
0	1	.	0	2	3

```
    2 . 0 2 1
 +  3 . 2 0 0
  ───────────
    5 . 2 2 1
```

Example

$4.1 \times 0.9 = ?$

$4.1 \times 0.9 = (41 \div 10) \times (9 \div 10) = 41 \times 9 \div 10 \div 10 = 369 \div 100 =$ **3.69**

Or

$41 \times 9 = 369$

$4.1 \times 0.9 \approx 4 \times 1 = 4$

So answer = **3.69**

- To **divide** decimals, you should make the number you are dividing by into a whole number.

Example

$2.79 \div 0.9 = ?$

Multiply both numbers by 10 (this is like equivalent fractions; what you do to one number you must do to the other): $27.9 \div 9$

You can now calculate the answer: **3.1**

Rounding Decimals

- Rounding decimals can help you to estimate answers to check your calculations.
- Rounding to one decimal place means rounding to the nearest 0.1 or $\frac{1}{10}$, so 12.74 rounded to one decimal place is 12.7
- Rounding to two decimal places means rounding to the nearest $\frac{1}{100}$, so 1.275 rounded to two decimal places is 1.28

Remember

The value 5 in a number is always rounded up.

Simple Probability

- Probability is how likely that something (an 'outcome') will happen.
- The probability that an outcome **will** happen and the probability it **will not** happen always add up to 1.
- You can describe the outcome with words such as impossible, unlikely, even chance, certain.
- You can also describe the outcome using numbers:
  - **Impossible** is represented by 0
  - **Even chance** is represented by 0.5
  - **Certain** is represented by 1.
- When you flip a coin, there are two possible outcomes. The possibility of flipping a head will be one chance in two. You can represent this as the fraction $\frac{1}{2}$, the decimal 0.5, or the percentage 50%.
- You can use probabilities to estimate how many times an outcome will happen.

Calculating Probability with Fractions

- To calculate a probability when all the outcomes are equally likely is straightforward. Simply add up the number of different outcomes and the total will be the fraction's denominator and the numerator will be 1.
- When the outcomes are not equally likely, calculate them as a numerical fraction, as follows.

Example

In a paper bag there are 4 strawberry, 3 orange, 2 lemon and 1 blackberry sweets. What is the probability of picking out a strawberry sweet?

First you need to work out the total number of sweets. Add together the numbers of each flavour sweet: 4 + 3 + 2 + 1 = 10 This provides the denominator for a fraction. Then each number of sweets provides the numerators.

The probability of picking a strawberry sweet is: $\frac{4}{10} = \frac{2}{5}$

Calculating Probability with Decimals and Percentages

- Probability can also be represented by decimals and percentages.

Example

What is the probability of this spinner landing on a 3?

There are five equal sections; the probability of landing on each of these equals 0.2.

Count the number of sections that have the number 3. There are three sections, so: 0.2 × 3 = 0.6

The probability of the spinner landing on 3 is **0.6** (or, as a percentage, **60%**).

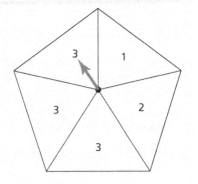

Problem Solving

- A number machine can be a good way to help visualise a multi-step fractions problem.

Example

A number machine is set up as follows:

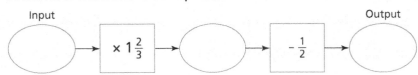

A number 2 is placed in the input. What will the output be?

$$1\frac{2}{3} = \frac{1 \times 3 + 2}{3} = \frac{5}{3}$$

$$\frac{2}{1} \times \frac{5}{3} = \frac{2 \times 5}{1 \times 3} = \frac{10}{3} \quad \boxed{\text{work out} \times 1\frac{2}{3}}$$

$$\frac{10}{3} - \frac{1}{2} = \frac{20}{6} - \frac{3}{6} \quad \boxed{\text{work out} - \frac{1}{2}}$$

$$\frac{20 - 3}{6} = \frac{17}{6} = 2\frac{5}{6}$$

- The context can vary, so try to look beyond the words to see the mathematics and pick out the calculation to be done.

Example

Boris has a bag containing 56 marbles. The marbles are either red, green, or blue. $\frac{3}{7}$ of the marbles are red. 25% of the remaining marbles are green. What is the probability of getting a blue marble if picked randomly from the bag?

$\frac{3}{7}$ of 56 = 56 ÷ 7 × 3 = 24	There are 24 red marbles.
56 – 24 = 32	There are 32 marbles that are either green or blue.
25% of 32 = 32 ÷ 4 = 8	There are 8 green marbles.
32 – 8 = 24	There are 24 blue marbles. (Check: 24 + 8 + 24 = 56)

There are 24 blue marbles out of a total 56 marbles, so the blue marbles are $\frac{24}{56} = \frac{3}{7}$ of the whole bag (this is the same as the proportion of red marbles).

The probability of randomly picking a blue marble is $\frac{3}{7}$.

Quick Test

1. Find the smallest of these quantities.

    A 1.8%   B 0.18   C $\frac{1}{18}$ D 0.081   E 0.108

2. Which of these is closest to 1?

    A 0.99   B 95%   C 1.05   D 103%   E $\frac{49}{50}$

3. Which of these does not have the same value as the others?

    A $\frac{1}{5}$ B 0.2   C 2%   D $\frac{2}{10}$ E $\frac{5}{25}$

4. What percentage of this grid is shaded?

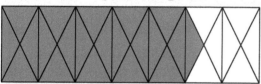

5. This spinner is equally likely to land on any of the numbers 1, 4, 9, 16 or 25. What is the probability that it will land on an odd number?

Ratio and Proportion

You should be able to:

- work out equivalent ratios
- divide numbers and quantities into a given ratio
- use proportional reasoning to solve problems
- solve percentage problems.

Ratios and Equivalent Ratios

- Ratios are a way of comparing numbers and quantities.
- A ratio shows proportion in a different way to a fraction.
- When you mix paint one part white to four parts blue, you write it as a ratio 1:4 so there is a total of five 'parts'. One part is white and four parts are blue. So the fraction of white paint is $\frac{1}{5}$ and the fraction of blue paint is $\frac{4}{5}$.
- As with fractions, where the denominator and numerator are multiplied or divided by the same number, the same rule applies to ratios:
  - These equivalent fractions are all produced by multiplying by 2: $\frac{1}{2} = \frac{2}{4} = \frac{4}{8}$
  - These equivalent ratios are all produced by multiplying by 2: 2:3 = 4:6 = 8:12

Remember

In ratios, always check which way round the numbers go. If two teaspoons of chilli are used to 100 g of mince, don't add 100 g of chilli to two teaspoons of mince!

Scales on Maps

- Maps, models and plans use scaling to enable something big to be represented on something much smaller.
- Maps, models and plans use space and distance on a smaller scale than in real life, but the relative position of objects stays the same. So a distance that is twice as long as another distance in real life will still be twice as long on the map.
- Scales are given as a ratio. A 1:500 ratio means that 1 centimetre on the map represents 500 cm (or 5 metres) in real life.

Remember

If given a measurement on a map, multiply to find the real distance.

If given a distance in real life, divide to find the distance on the map.

Example

Gwen draws a map to show her route to school. She uses a scale of 1:40 000.

a) Her school is 2 km away from her house. How far will it be on the map?

2 km = 2000 m = 200 000 cm   200 000 ÷ 40 000 = 5

On the map the school will be **5 cm** away.

b) Gwen has put a spot on the map where the swimming pool is. On the map the distance from her house to the swimming pool is 8.5 cm. How far away is it in real life?

8.5 cm × 40 000 = 340 000 cm

(this isn't very useful as it is hard to understand how far 340 000 cm is)

340 000 cm = 3400 m = 3.4 km

In real life the swimming pool is **3.4 km** away.

Proportion

- You can divide numbers and quantities into a given ratio.
  First you need to work out how many parts there are in total.

Example

A field contains 28 llamas. These are then split between two fields in a ratio of 2:5. How many llamas are in each field?

To solve this problem:

- there are seven (2 + 5) equal 'groups' of llamas
- to find out how many in a group, divide the total number by the number of groups: $28 \div 7 = 4$
- to finish the problem, multiply this figure by the number of groups on each side of the ratio.
  $4 \times 2 = 8$ $4 \times 5 = 20$

The number of llamas in each field is **8** and **20**.

- Knowing the proportions of one quantity to another means that if one quantity changes, you can work out the other.

Example

In a recipe you need two eggs to every 300g of sugar. How many eggs will you need if the recipe asks for 1200g of sugar?

To solve this problem:

- first look for the proportions you are dealing with
  2:300 is the ratio of eggs to sugar (in grams)   ?:1200
- you now need to work out how many times bigger 1200 is than 300: $1200 \div 300 = 4$
- so to calculate the new quantity, multiply the original number of eggs by 4: $2:300 \times 4$

The answer is **8** eggs.

Percentage Calculations

- Some percentage calculations are quite simple if you look for alternative methods to solve them. Using equivalents by converting a percentage to a fraction can speed up your calculations.

Example

Find 10% of £350.

10% is the same as $\frac{1}{10}$

So 10% of £350 equals **£35**.

- Working backwards can help solve some questions. In this case, you don't need to convert the percentage to a fraction; just look for simple fractions.

Example

Find 75% of £350.

Find half (50%) of £350, then find half of this half (25%), then add the two together:

£350 $\div$ 2 = £175   £175 $\div$ 2 = £87.50

£175 + £87.50 = **£262.50**

- Use multiplication and division to solve percentage problems when you know the total amount.
- If you can find 1% of an amount, you can multiply this value to find any percentage. To find 1% you need to divide the number by 100 – move the digits two places to the right. So 1% of £451 is £4.51
- To find 10% of any number, move the digits one place to the right. So 10% of £451 is £45.10
- Once you know 1% and 10%, many calculations are simple. So 5% of £451 is £45.10 ÷ 2 = £22.55

Example

Find 14% of £451.

Either multiply 14 by 1%: £4.51 × 14 = **£63.14**

Or add 10% and 5% and subtract 1%:

£45.10 + £22.55 − £4.51 = **£63.14**

- You can also use multiplication and division to solve percentage problems when you need to find the total amount.

Example

48 children stay for homework club after school. If this is 24% of the school, how many children are in the whole school?

To solve this, you still need to find 1%. If 48 children are 24% of the school, to find 1% divide 48 by 24:

48 ÷ 24 = 2

Then multiply this by 100:   2 × 100 = 200

So there are **200** children in the school.

> **Remember**
>
> Once you find 1% of a total, or 10% of a total, you can use these values to work out other percentage amounts such as 5% and 2.5%.

> **Remember**
>
> Always check what the percentage is out of. 50% of 560 is smaller than 5% of 56 000:
>
> 50% of 560 = 280, but 5% of 56 000 = 2800

Quick Test

1. Which of these ratios is not equivalent to 16:12?
   A 20:15   B 8:6   C 24:16   D 36:27   E 32:24
2. In a choir, the ratio of boys to girls is 5:3. There are 18 girls in the choir. How many children are in the choir altogether?
3. Will has just finished building a model plane with a scale of 1:72. The model is 20 cm long. How long is the real plane in metres?
4. St Mark's School sold 500 tickets for a raffle. 4% of the tickets won a prize. How many tickets did not win a prize?
5. Which answer is different from the others?
   A 50% of £50   B 25% of £100   C $\frac{5}{8}$ of £40   D 30% of £75   E 10% of £250
6. A jar of jam used to cost £1.20 but the price has increased by 20%. What does it cost now?

Algebra

You should be able to:

- understand and use algebraic notation
- solve equations
- understand sequences and work out missing patterns or terms
- work out how many different combinations are possible in a given situation.

Understanding Algebraic Notation

- You need to know how additions, subtractions, multiplications and divisions are written in algebra.
- To add and subtract, write the letters as you would do for numbers in a calculation.

Example
Adding a to b: $\quad\quad\quad\quad a + b =$
Subtracting a from b: $\quad\quad b - a =$

- Multiplication sums do not use signs; the numbers and letters are written next to each other.

Example
$4x$ is four times the value of x, so if $x = 6$ then:
$4x = 4 \times 6 = \mathbf{24}$

- Division sums are usually shown like numerical fractions.

Example
$\frac{k}{10}$ means the number represented by k should be divided by 10.
So if $k = 40$, then:
$\frac{k}{10} = \frac{40}{10} = 40 \div 10 = \mathbf{4}$

Using Substitution and Solving Equations

- Substituting letters for unknown numbers helps to solve equations.

Example
$8 + ? + ? = 26$
There are a variety of answers that could be correct.

$8 + 1 + 17 = 26$	$8 + 2 + 16 = 26$
$8 + 3 + 15 = 26$	$8 + 4 + 14 = 26$
$8 + 5 + 13 = 26$	$8 + 6 + 12 = 26$, etc.

Using letters to replace the ?: $\quad\quad 8 + a + a = 26$
You can then work out the value of a. You will also understand that a needs to have the same value each time it occurs within this equation. So $a = \mathbf{9}$.

- You can solve equations in two different ways – by simplifying the sums until you find the answer, or by using number machines.

Simplifying the Sum

- To solve equations by simplifying the sum, you need to move the numbers you know to one side of the equation, leaving the calculations involving letters you don't know on the other side.
- You can move a number from one side of the equation to the other by using inverse operations.

Example

$k = 3s + 4$

If you know $k = 19$, you can work out the value of s:

$19 = 3s + 4$

$19 - 4 = 3s$

$15 = 3s$

$15 \div 3 = s$, so $s = 5$

Using Number Machines

- Use inverse operations when you work backwards.

Example

Look at this number machine for the equation $\frac{4b + 4}{2} = 12$

What is the value of b?

$b \rightarrow \boxed{\times 4} \rightarrow \boxed{+ 4} \rightarrow \boxed{\div 2} \rightarrow \boxed{12}$

First change the direction and the operations:

$b \leftarrow \boxed{\div 4} \leftarrow \boxed{- 4} \leftarrow \boxed{\times 2} \leftarrow \boxed{12}$

Then complete the operations: $b = 5$

> **Remember**
>
> The unknown value can occur more than once in the equation, e.g.
>
> $2x + 3 = x + 7$
>
> $(x = 4)$
>
> And the answer can be a fraction:
>
> $16x = 4$
>
> $x = \frac{1}{4}$

> **Remember**
>
> Make sure you change the operation when you change direction.

Recognising Sequences

- You need to be able to spot number sequences quickly.
- Odd and even numbers:
  - Both odd and even number sequences have a difference of 2 each time.
  - Even numbers are all multiples of 2.

  1 **2** 3 **4** 5 **6** 7 **8** 9 **10** ...

- Sequences from multiplication tables:
  - Equal differences indicate a repeated addition sequence.

    6   12   18   24
       +6   +6   +6

  - Increasing differences can indicate a sequence linked by multiplication. This pattern shows multiplication by 2.

    2   4   8   16
       +2   +4   +8

  - Decreasing numbers can indicate repeated subtraction or division.

- Make sure you can recognise sequences of square and cube numbers:

  Square numbers: 1   4   9   16   25   36   ...
  Cube numbers: 1   8   27   64   125   216   ...

- Triangular numbers start at 1 and then add 2, 3, 4 progressively. The differences are consecutive numbers.

  1   3   6   10   15   21   ...

- Prime numbers are only divisible by 1 and themselves; there is no pattern to them.

  2   3   5   7   11   13   ...

- If the sequence is not easy to recognise, look at the differences between the numbers. This can help to identify patterns.

  7   8   11   16   23
     +1   +3   +5   +7

- Look out for sequences that go backwards as well as forwards.

Completing and Extending Sequences

- First check the pattern in the sequence by looking at the differences between your given numbers.

Example

Work out the missing number in this sequence:

8   **16**   **___**   **32**   **40**   **48**

The example here is a positive number sequence. The difference between the given numbers is always 8.
Work out the difference between the terms given, then add/subtract this to a number next to the gap.
Check that your answer fits the sequence correctly.
Here 16 + 8 or 32 – 8 will give the correct answer of **24**.

> **Remember**
>
> If the sequence is negative, the process shown in the example to the left is reversed.

Shape-based Patterns

- Identify what stays the same in the pattern and what changes.

Example

What is the next shape in the series?

o   o   o   o
o   oo   ooo   oooo

First find the things that stay the same. Here these are the shape and the top row.

Then find out the element that changes: one circle is added to the bottom row each time.

So the next shape is: o
              ooooo

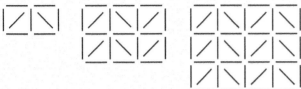
Two Unknowns

- When dealing with a situation where there are two unknown values, try to set up equations with the information that is given.
- You may be able to rule out some multiple-choice options straight away and then test the others.

Example

James is making button pictures. Each rainbow picture he makes uses 10 red buttons. Each fish picture he makes has 6 red buttons. He makes p rainbow pictures and enjoys making the fish pictures even more so makes q fish pictures. He started with 50 red buttons but only has 6 left when he is finished. Which is the correct solution?

A $p = 2, q = 1$ **B** $p = 3, q = 5$ **C** $p = 2, q = 4$

D $p = 3, q = 3$ **E** $p = 1, q = 6$

Start by writing down the information from the question mathematically.

$q > p$ q is bigger than p

$10p + 6q = 50 - 6 = 44$

Using this information, test the answer options:

It is not **A** or **D**, because q is not bigger than p in those answers.

Try **B**: $10 \times 3 + 6 \times 5 = 60$ This is not the right answer; we want it to be 44.

Try **C**: $10 \times 2 + 6 \times 4 = 44$ This is the right answer.

Try **E**: $10 \times 1 + 6 \times 6 = 46$ This is close but not right – this way he would only have 4 buttons left.

Option **C** is correct.

Combinations and Permutations

- Combinations and permutations are all about how many different ways a set of items can be put together.
- Often the best way to attempt these questions is to write down one item (use a code, like the first letter, to make it easier to do) and then all the things that could go with it. The question will explain how the matching up can happen.

Example
A café offers the sandwich fillings shown on the right.
How many different options are there for a sandwich with two fillings?

Ham (H), Cheese (C), Tuna (T), Salad (S), Hummus (M)

There are the following possible combinations:

HC	CT	TS	SM
HT	CS	TM	(SC = CS, SH = HS, ST = TS, so all covered)
HS	CM	(Tuna with either Ham or Cheese is already covered)	
HM	(CH = HC so is not included again)		

There are **10** possible combinations.

Notice that if there are five items on the list, the first item could match with all four of the other items. The second item matches with the three remaining items but has already been matched with the first item, etc. So for five items to be arranged into different pairs the calculation becomes 4 + 3 + 2 + 1 = 10. Sometimes it might be possible to have two of the same, so in this situation you might get HH, CC, TT, SS, MM.

- Sometimes there will be two lists so each item from one list can go with one item from the second list.

Example
A café offers a (single filling) sandwich with a piece of fruit as part of a meal deal. How many different combinations of sandwich and fruit are possible?

List the possible combinations:

HA	CA	TA	SA
HB	CB	TB	SB
HC	CC	TC	SC
HG	CG	TG	SG

Counting up there are **16** possible combinations.

- The answer above is set out as a grid with each item from the first list having a column and each item from the second list having a row. This means the number of possible combinations is 4 × 4 = 16. If there were 5 sandwich filling options and 6 types of fruit, the number of combinations would be 30. Can you see why?

- In both of the previous examples the order of the items doesn't matter – they are **combinations**.
- **Permutations** are when the order does matter, for example the numbers on the code for a safe. If you knew it had the digits 390 but didn't know the order, that still leaves a lot of different numbers. Sometimes digits or items can be repeated but sometimes they cannot – think about the practical situation to decide.

Remember

Make sure you have a system when listing outcomes. Start with the first and list all the possible things that could go with it, then move on to the second. Grids can be a helpful way of keeping track of what you have done and help you to spot patterns.

Example

Four people (Anand, Beatrice, Charlie, Damien) are running a race. How many different permutations could there be for the medal positions (i.e. the first three places)?

List the first three in order of finishing. Have a system: here the columns have the same pair first, and they are always done from earlier in the alphabet first.

| ABC | ACB | ADB | BAC | BCA | BDA |
| ABD | ACD | ADC | BAD | BCD | BDC |

Having got this far it is possible to spot a pattern, which can save you writing out all the different permutations. For each different person in first place there are six possible permutations for the remaining runners.

So, there are 4 × 6 = **24** permutations for the medal positions.

Quick Test

1. Maya is planting sunflower seeds. She plants m seeds in each small pot and n seeds in each big pot. When she has planted 4 of each size pot, she has 4 seeds left over from a packet of 20. Which is correct?

   A $m = 2, n = 1$ B $m = 3, n = 2$ C $m = 2, n = 3$ D $m = 1, n = 4$ E $m = 1, n = 3$

2. When playing a game, these two spinners are spun at the same time and the two values obtained are added together. How many different combinations of totals are there?

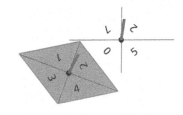

Measurement

You should be able to:

- understand and use measures such as money, time, temperature, speed, length, capacity and mass (weight)
- convert between different units of measurement
- calculate the area, volume and perimeter of different shapes.

Money

- Money is measured in pounds (£) and pence (p).
- There are 100 pence in £1, so 3p written in pounds would be represented in the hundredths column, i.e. £0.03.
- We have these coins and notes in the UK: 1p, 2p, 5p, 10p, 20p, 50p, £1, £2, £5, £10, £20, £50.
- You can make any amount of money from the coins and notes.

Example
Gareth has these coins:

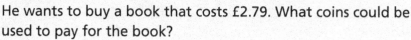

He wants to buy a book that costs £2.79. What coins could be used to pay for the book?

Using the two £1 coins leaves £0.79 or 79p to pay.

Using the 50p piece leaves 29p.

Using a 20p piece leaves 9p.

Using the 5p piece leaves 4p, which can be made using the 2p and 2 × 1p.

£2.79 = £1 + £1 + 50p + 20p + 5p + 2p + 1p + 1p

- You need to be able to calculate using money.

Example
Misa gets two 20 pence pieces for pocket money every week. She puts them in her money box. After how many weeks will she have more than £5?

It is easier to work in pence here:

£5 = 500p and Misa gets 40p each week.

$500 \div 40 = 50 \div 4 = 25 \div 2 = 12.5$

Now round up 12.5 to the next whole week.

So it will take **13** weeks for Misa to have more than £5 in her money box.

Time

- If you are working with the 12-hour clock, you need to understand am and pm. For example, 9.34 am is in the morning and 9.34 pm is in the evening.
- If you are working with the 24-hour clock, you always use four numbers. So 09:34 indicates the time is in the morning, while 21:34 is in the evening (9.34 pm).
- When converting 12-hour clock times to 24-hour clock times, take care when dealing with times from 12 midnight (00:00 on the 24-hour clock) to 12.59 am (00:59).
- When asked to work out the difference between two times (a time interval), it is useful to quickly draw a timeline.
- If the time interval crosses 12 noon or 12 midnight, you can use extra steps to make the calculation easier.

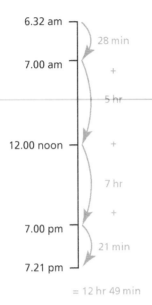

Calculating with Time and Using Timetables

- To calculate using time, you need to know the units used to measure time:

1 millennium	1000 years
1 century	100 years
1 decade	10 years
1 year	12 months or 365 days (but 366 days in a leap year)
1 day	24 hours
1 hour	60 minutes
1 minute	60 seconds

- To remember how many days there are in each month, you can use your knuckles.
- The raised knuckles have 31 days, and the indents between the knuckles have 30 days, except for February, which has 28 days (but has 29 days in a leap year).

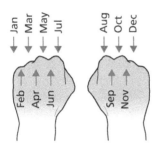

Example
Tennis lessons are 45 minutes long. If Janine's grandparents offer to pay for 15 hours of lessons, how many lessons can Janine take?

There are two ways to solve this problem.
If you double 45 minutes, this makes 90 minutes
(1 hour 30 minutes) which is the time needed for 2 lessons.
4 lessons = 3 hours
Multiplying by 5 gives:
20 lessons = 15 hours
Therefore, number of lessons in 15 hours = **20**

Alternatively, you can start by calculating the total number of minutes in 15 hours:

15 hours = 15 × 60 minutes = 900 minutes
Dividing by 45 minutes per lesson gives **20** lessons.

- Timetables (bus, rail) usually use the 24-hour clock. They are displayed in columns and rows.
- Each column represents a separate journey. If there is a blank space or dash in a timetable, it means that there isn't a service at that stop.

Example

What is the earliest train you can catch from Jamestone to Seeford on Monday?

Station		Saturdays only		
Jamestone	05:34	07:34	08:34	13:34
Seeford		07:42	08:42	13:42
Lingtop	06:34	08:34		14:34
Strayram	06:54	08:54	09:54	14:54

The earliest train is at **08:34** (as the 07:34 only runs on a Saturday).

Temperature

- Temperature measures how warm, or cold, something is.
- The unit measure of temperature is degrees Celsius (°C).
- A thermometer is used to measure the temperature of something.
- Values below 0°C are represented by negative numbers.

Example

Emma checks the temperature in her greenhouse in August and the thermometer displays the reading shown.
On the coldest winter day, the temperature is 43°C colder. What is the temperature on the coldest day?

36 − 43 = −7, so on the coldest winter day the temperature was **−7°C**.

Units of Measure

- You need to know what unit is suitable for measuring different things and have a sense of the size of each unit.

Item	Type of Measure	Measuring Equipment	Units of Measurement
How heavy a grown up is	Weight (mass)	Bathroom scales	Kilograms (kg) (Imperial units: stones and ounces)
Size of a book	Length	Ruler	Centimetres (cm) (Imperial units: inches)
Milk	Capacity (volume)	Measuring jug	Litres (l) or millilitres (ml) (Imperial units: pints)
Size of a room	Length	Tape measure	Metres (m) (Imperial units: feet and inches)
How much flour when baking	Weight (mass)	Kitchen scales	Grams (g) (Imperial units: pounds and ounces)
Dose of medicine	Capacity (volume)	Medical syringe or measuring spoon	Millilitres (ml)
Distance of a bike ride	Length	Pedometer; measuring wheel; using an app; distance from a scaled map	Kilometres (km) (Imperial units: miles)

Converting Between Metric Units

- Metric units function on a system in base 10, which means there are set units and prefixes (the bit at the beginning of a unit) that tell us how big or small the unit is.
- The prefixes are:
    - milli- (meaning a 'thousandth'), e.g. millimetres (mm), milligrams (mg), millilitres (ml)
    - centi- (meaning a 'hundredth'), e.g. centimetres (cm), centilitres (cl)
    - kilo- (meaning 1000 times bigger), e.g. kilometres (km), kilograms (kg).
- When multiplying or adding measures, it is sometimes more sensible to convert units.

> **Remember**
>
> The three standard units (known as SI units) are:
> - metres (m) for length
> - grams (g) for weight (or mass)
> - litres (l) for capacity (or volume).

Example

Seren is building a tower with bricks that are 15 cm tall. Before toppling, the tower is 22 blocks high. What was the maximum height of Seren's tower?

A 330 m   **B** 0.33 m   **C** 3300 m   **D** 3.3 m   **E** 33 m

$15 \times 22 = 30 \times 11 = 330$ cm

To match it to the answer, convert into metres.

$330 \div 100 = 3.3$ m (option **D**)

Check the answer makes sense. Try converting back or using an estimation to make sure, as it is very easy to make a mistake and multiply instead of divide or vice-versa.

> **Remember**
>
> There are:
> - 1000 millilitres (or 1000 cm³) in a litre
> - 100 cm in a metre
> - 1000 g in a kilogram
> - 1000 kg in a tonne.

- Take extra care when working with different units of area or volume:
    - $1\,m^2 = 1\,m \times 1\,m = 100\,cm \times 100\,cm = 10\,000\,cm^2$
    - $1\,cm^3 = 1\,cm \times 1\,cm \times 1\,cm = 10\,mm \times 10\,mm \times 10\,mm = 1000\,mm^3$

Imperial-to-Metric Conversions

- The most common conversions are:
    - miles to kilometres
    - pints or gallons to litres
    - pounds to kilograms.

> **Remember**
>
> These imperial-to-metric conversions are approximate.

Length

Imperial	1 inch	1 foot	39 inches	1 mile	5 miles
Metric	2.5 cm	30 cm	1 m	1.6 km	8 km

Weight / Mass

Imperial	1 ounce (oz)	1 pound (lb)	2.2 pounds	1 stone	1 ton
Metric	28 g	450 g	1 kg	6.4 kg	1 tonne

Capacity / Volume

Imperial	1 fluid ounce	1 pint	1.75 pints	1 gallon
Metric	30 ml	600 ml	1 litre	4.5 litres

Reading Scales

- When reading scales, first establish what each division stands for:
  - count the gaps (not the lines!) in between the numbers given on the scale
  - subtract the two numbers from each other
  - divide the result by the number of gaps.

Example

What is the reading shown on these weighing scales?

To work out the scale:
- first look at the larger divisions, e.g. 4–5 kg
- subtract the smaller from the larger: 1 kg
- divide this by the number of spaces, making sure you know the units you are using.

So: 1 kg ÷ 5 = 0.2 kg or 1000 g ÷ 5 = 200 g
The value indicated on the scale is **4.2 kg** or **4 kg 200 g**.

Perimeter and Circumference

- The **perimeter** is the distance around the outside of a 2D shape (like fencing around the edge of a garden).

Example

A regular pentagon has a perimeter of 65 cm. What is the length of one side?

Remember
Knowing the properties of 2D shapes will help solve perimeter problems.

A pentagon has five sides, so to find the length of one side divide the total perimeter by 5.

65 cm ÷ 5 = **13 cm**

- If you are given measurements in different units (such as centimetres and metres), change them so that they are the same before you start your calculations.

Example

Find the perimeter of the shape shown right.

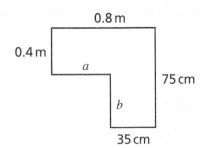

First convert all the measurement to centimetres:

40 cm   80 cm   75 cm   35 cm

Then calculate the measurements of a and b.

To find a: 80 cm – 35 cm = 45 cm
To find b: 75 cm – 40 cm = 35 cm

Now add together all the measurements to find the total perimeter:

40 cm + 80 cm + 75 cm + 35 cm + 35 cm + 45 cm = **310 cm**

- The perimeter of a circle is called the **circumference** (C).
- The circumference can be calculated using the formula:
  $C = \pi \times 2 \times$ radius, or equivalently, $C = \pi \times$ diameter
- The diameter of a circle is twice its radius.

- The value of π (Greek letter 'pi') is slightly more than 3 and it stays the same whatever the size of the circle.

Example

Alison is taking her baby for a walk in a buggy and wants to know how far it is to the park. The back wheel has a circumference of 80 cm. The wheel does 600 revolutions to get to the park. How far away is the park?

80 cm = 0.8 m

0.8 × 600 = 8 × 60 = 48 × 10 = **480 m**

Quick Test

1. How should the time 4.45 in the afternoon be written?
   A 14:45   B 16:45   C 18:45   D 04:45   E 15:45
2. At the cinema, the adverts and trailers last 25 minutes and the main film lasts 1 hour and 40 minutes, with a five-minute gap in between.
   If the whole programme starts at 3.20 pm, what time does it finish?
3. At the swimming pool where Simone swims, you pay £3 per hour to use the pool. Simone goes to twelve 40-minute sessions in a month. How much does this cost?
4. Emily is weighing ingredients for a cake. The scale currently shows the weight below.
   She needs to add 800 g dried fruit to the mixture.
   What will the scale read after she adds it?
   A 1.48 kg   B 1.804 kg   C 2 kg   D 2.2 kg   E 2.4 kg
5. A baby girl drinks 600 ml of milk each day. How many litres of milk does she drink in a week?

Area and Volume

- The area is the surface of a 2D shape.
- Area is measured in units squared, e.g. mm², cm², m².

Rectangle or Square	Parallelogram	Triangle	Circle
Area = Length × Width	Area = Base × Perpendicular height	Area = $\frac{1}{2}$ (Base × Height)	Area = π × Radius²

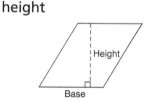

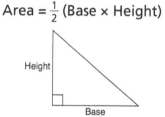

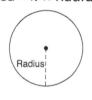

- You can work out the surface area of a 3D shape by adding together the areas of each individual face.
- 3D shapes have volume (the amount of space inside the shape).
- Volume is measured in units cubed, e.g. mm³, cm³, m³.

Cuboid	Prism or Cylinder
Volume = Length × Width × Height	Volume = Area of cross-section × Length

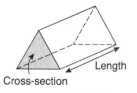

Remember

The perpendicular height is the shortest distance from the base of the shape to the top; this is **not** the height of a slanted side.

Speed

- Speed is the measure of how distance changes relative to time. If talking about how fast a car travels, we might say it goes at 30 miles per hour (mph). In other words, every hour the car would travel 30 miles.
- At other times speed may be measured metrically in kilometres per hour (kph or km/h) or metres per second (m/s).
- The 'per' means divide. Divide the distance travelled (km) by the time it has taken (hours) to find a speed in kilometres per hour.
- If a speed is known and you want to find the distance, you do the inverse function and multiply by the time taken.
- If you want to find out how long it took to go a certain distance at a set speed, divide the distance travelled by the speed.

Example
A train travels at 50 m/s for 3 minutes. How far does it travel in this time in km?

3 minutes = 3 × 60 = 180 s
50 × 180 = 9000 m = **9 km**

Example
A cyclist takes two and a half hours to travel 30 miles.
a) Assuming the cyclist went at a constant speed, how fast was she travelling?
   30 ÷ 2.5 = **12 mph**
b) How long would it take her to travel 18 miles at the same speed?
   18 ÷ 12 = 1.5
   It would take **1 hour 30 minutes**.

Problem Solving

- Problem-solving questions about measure will generally need more than one step to solve.

Example
A builder is tiling a kitchen floor using tiles that are 20 cm by 30 cm. Boxes of tiles cost £32 each and contain 25 tiles. The kitchen floor is a rectangle measuring 2 m by 3.5 m. How much will it cost to buy enough tiles for the kitchen floor?

Answer planning: What is the area of the kitchen floor? (Area of rectangle: $l \times w$)
How many m² does each box of tiles cover? (Remember to convert into m)
How many boxes are needed? (Divide floor by area from a box, round up)
How much will that cost? (Multiply the number of boxes by 32)

Area of kitchen floor = 2 × 3.5 = 7 m²
A tile is 0.2 × 0.3 = 0.06 m²
A box of tiles covers 0.06 × 25 = 1.5 m²
How many boxes? 7 ÷ 1.5 = 4 remainder 1
This means you need more than 4 boxes, so 5 boxes need to be bought.
How much will the tiles cost?   5 × 32 = **£160**

Example

Cara has a long piece of rope. She wraps it around two identical posts that are stuck in the ground, as shown in the diagram. When it has gone around the posts five times, the remaining rope measures 55 cm. How long is the rope?

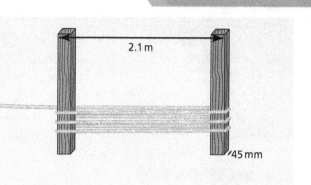

First convert everything into metres:

45 mm = 0.045 m   55 cm = 0.55 m

For one time around the posts:

2.1 + 0.045 + 2.1 + 0.045 = 4.29 m of rope

Five times around the posts = 4.29 × 5

$\qquad\qquad\qquad\qquad$ = 42.9 ÷ 2 = 21.45 m

Total length of rope = 21.45 + 0.55 = **22 m**

Quick Test

1. Find:
   a) the volume of this cuboid in cubic centimetres
   b) the surface area in square centimetres.

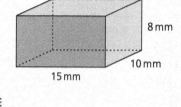

2. Two of these shapes have the same area. Which are they?

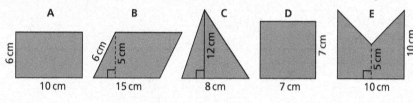

   A B and E   B A and B   C C and D   D C and E   E A and C

3. How many copies of the small rectangle would fill up the space inside the large shape?

4. There are two routes between Sian's house and her Grandma's. The first route is 14 miles and the average speed for the journey is 28 mph. The second route is 20 miles.
   If both routes take the same length of time, what is the average speed for the second route?

5. Zak is building a cuboidal pond in his garden for his 15 fish. Each fish needs to have 45 litres of water to avoid overcrowding. 1 m³ = 1000 litres. The fish also need the water to have a minimum depth of 3 ft (use 1 ft = 30 cm).
   How many more fish could Zak buy to put in his pond if the depth is the minimum 3 ft?

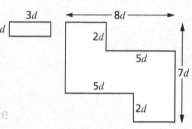
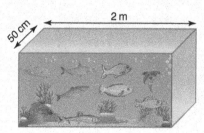

   A 0   B 2   C 5   D 10   E 11

Geometry

You should be able to:

- recall and apply the properties of common 2D and 3D shapes
- reflect and rotate shapes
- relate nets to 3D shapes and solve spatial reasoning problems
- solve problems involving angles, including within 2D shapes and in terms of direction or rotation
- work with co-ordinates and find missing points.

2D Shapes

- 2D shapes are flat and so have just two dimensions (width and length). They can be classified in a number of ways.

> **Remember**
>
> Regular polygons are 2D shapes with equal sides and equal angles.

Shapes with curved sides	Circle • One side • Infinite lines of symmetry	Semi-circle • Two sides • One line of symmetry

Shapes with three sides	Equilateral triangle	Right-angled triangle	Isosceles triangle	Scalene triangle
Sides	All equal	Longest side is opposite the right angle	Two equal sides	No equal sides
Angles	All equal (60°)	One right angle	Two base angles are equal	No equal angles
Lines of symmetry	3	1 (if the two sides next to the right angle are of equal length) or 0	1	0

Shapes with four sides (quadrilaterals)	Square	Rectangle	Parallelogram
Sides	All equal	Two pairs of equal sides	Two pairs of equal sides
Angles	All equal (90°)	All equal (90°)	Opposite angles are equal
Lines of symmetry	4	2	0
Pairs of parallel sides	2	2	2

> **Remember**
>
> Other 2D shapes include pentagons (five sides), hexagons (six sides), octagons (eight sides) and decagons (ten sides).

More quadrilaterals	Rhombus	Trapezium	Kite
Sides	All equal	No equal sides (but an isosceles trapezium does have one pair of equal sides)	Two pairs of equal sides that are next to each other
Angles	Opposite angles are equal	An isosceles trapezium has two pairs of equal angles	One equal pair of angles
Lines of symmetry	2	1 (if two sides are of equal length) or 0	1
Pairs of parallel sides	2	1	0

3D Shapes

- 3D shapes are solid shapes with three dimensions (width, length and height). They usually have flat faces, straight edges and pointed vertices.

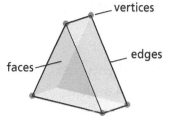

- Two of the most common 3D shapes are:
  - **prisms:** if you imagine slicing prisms like a loaf of bread, the faces remain the same shape and size
  - **pyramids**: these come to a point at the top, and if you slice them, the face stays the same shape but becomes smaller nearer to the top.
- Note that a hemisphere is a sphere cut in half, so it has one edge and two faces (one curved and one flat).
- The properties of some common 3D shapes are:

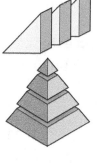

3D shape	Sphere	Cylinder	Cube	Cuboid	Triangular prism	Tetrahedron (triangular-based pyramid)	Square-based pyramid
Edges	0	2	12	12	9	6	8
Vertices	0	0	8	8	6	4	5
Faces	1	3	6	6	5	4	5

Types of Angle

- Angles are created when two straight lines meet or intersect.
- Angles on a straight line sum to 180°.
- Angles at a point sum to 360°.

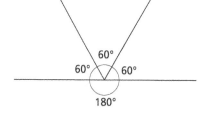

Acute angle	Right angle	Obtuse angle	Reflex angle
Makes less than a quarter turn (90°).	Makes a quarter turn (90°).	Makes more than a quarter turn (90°) but less than a half turn (180°).	Makes more than a half turn (180°).

Unknown Angles in Shapes

Angles in Triangles

- The interior angles of a triangle always add up to 180°. This means you can work out unknown angles.
- If a triangle contains a right angle and you know one of the other angles, you can find the third angle.
- Isosceles triangles have two equal sides (often marked with a single line through them) and therefore two equal angles.

Remember

Angles marked with a square, rather than an arc, indicate a right angle.

Example

Work out the value of the angle x.

Angles in a triangle sum to 180°.
The two base angles of this isosceles triangle both equal 43°.
$43° \times 2 = 86°$
So $x = 180 - 86 = $ **94°**

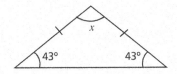

Angles in Quadrilaterals

- The interior angles of a quadrilateral always add up to 360°.
- Particular types of quadrilateral have extra properties:
    - Squares and rectangles have four equal angles of 90°.
    - Parallelograms and rhombuses have two pairs of opposite angles that are equal.
- If you know any of the angles in a parallelogram, you can work out the other three.
- Kites have two opposite angles that are equal.

Remember

A parallelogram is a 'pushed-over' rectangle and a rhombus is a 'pushed-over' square.

Example

In this kite, angle a is 90°and angle b is 100°.
Work out the values of angles c and d.

Angle c must be the same as b, so $c = $ **100°**
And therefore $d = 360 - (90 + 100 + 100) = $ **70°**

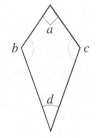

- When two shapes are joined together, use your knowledge of 2D shapes to help you work out the angles.

Example

If angle $a = 52°$ and angle $b = 43°$, work out all of the other angles.

Because angles a, b and c form a triangle: $c = 180° - (43° + 52°) = $ **85°**

We know $c + d = 180°$ (point on a straight line) so: $d = 180° - 85° = $ **95°**

As angles d, e, f, g form a rhombus, $f = d$, so: $e + g = 360° - (95° + 95°) = 170°$

Angles e and g are also equal so: $e = g = 170° \div 2 = $ **85°**

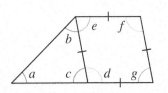

Symmetry, Reflection and Rotation

- A line of symmetry is often represented by a dashed line.
- In the lettering shown (right), A, C, D and T all have one line of symmetry. F has no lines of symmetry and O and H have two lines of symmetry. If the O was written as a perfect circle, it would have an infinite number of symmetry lines.
- Reflection is where a shape is formed using a line of symmetry as the 'mirror line'.

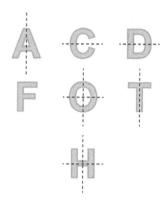

Example

Reflect each shape in the dashed line:

Diagonal lines tend to be a bit trickier to see how the shape will behave.

- **Rotational symmetry** is where the object can be placed in different positions, by rotating it, but still appear the same.

Example

There are five different ways this regular pentagon could fit back into the jigsaw space. A regular pentagon has rotational symmetry of order 5. (Note: the smiley face icon is used to show how the shape is being rotated).

Nets and 3D Spatial Reasoning

- A net is an 'unfolded' shape. A net can be folded in different ways to make a 3D shape.

Remember

You can think of rotational symmetry like a child's wooden jigsaw where the shape could fit in the hole in different ways. The order of rotational symmetry is how many ways the piece would fit back into the space as it was turned through 360°.

Remember

All of the shapes in a net form the faces of the shape. The net of a cube will be made of six identical squares.

3D shape	Examples of nets that work	Some examples of nets that wouldn't work
Cube	There are 11 possibilities.	
Cuboid		
Cylinder	A cylinder net is two circles for the ends and a rectangle which forms the tube part.	
Pyramid		

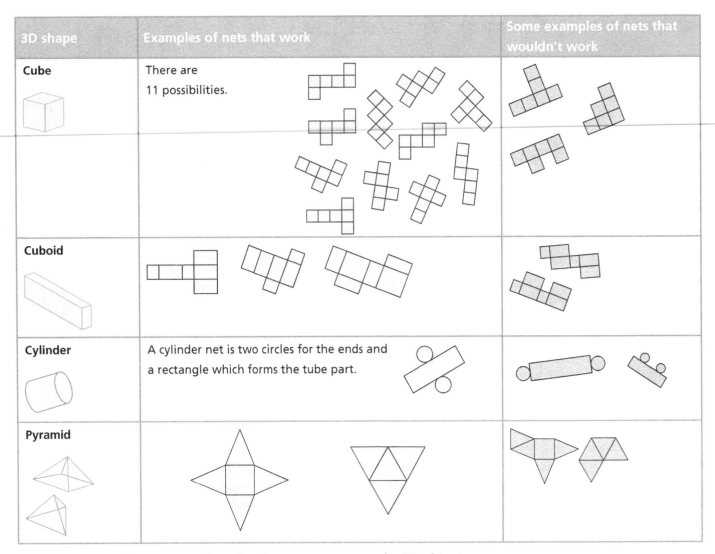

- You may need to use your imagination to move around a 3D object and think about what it would look like from different sides.

Example
Toby makes the building (shown right) out of toy blocks.
The image shows the front of his building.
Which picture shows the back of Toby's building?

A 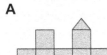   B    C    D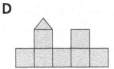

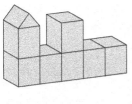

Imagine that you are standing behind the blocks and looking at them from that side. What would you see? The answer is **C**.

Compass Directions

- A compass is split into four main directions: North (N), South (S), East (E) and West (W).
- From any point, you can use a compass to define which way you are facing. If you face North and then turn 90° to your right

(clockwise), you will be facing East. Turn another 90° to the right and you will be facing South, and so on.

- Make sure you know the intermediate directions of North-East (NE), South-East (SE), South-West (SW) and North-West (NW).
- When facing North, a turn of 45° anti-clockwise turns you to NW.

Example

Carla is facing North-West and then turns anti-clockwise through 135°. Which compass direction is she facing now?

Drawing the compass points can be helpful. 135° = 90° + 45°

From NW, turning 135° anti-clockwise will take her to **South**.

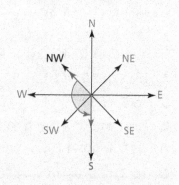

Co-ordinate Grids

- Using the scales on the two axes of a grid helps to locate points. Simple co-ordinates are shown on a positive grid:
  - There are two axes, x (horizontal) and y (vertical).
  - The x co-ordinate is always written before the y co-ordinate in the form (x, y).
- More complex co-ordinates are shown on grids arranged in four quadrants which include negative numbers.

> **Remember**
>
> The order in which you should read co-ordinates can be remembered by a plane taking off – it has to travel horizontally (x) down the runway before gaining (vertical) height (y).

Example

Triangle *ABC* is an isosceles triangle. If the co-ordinates for *A* are (3, 12) and the co-ordinates for *C* are (–3, –6), find the co-ordinates of *B*.

Draw in the line of symmetry for the isosceles triangle.

Mark the scale onto the y- and x-axis: each interval equals 3.
x-axis co-ordinate, four intervals between *C* and *B*: $-3 + (4 \times 3) = 9$
y-axis co-ordinate, six intervals between *A* and *B*: $12 - (6 \times 3) = -6$
The co-ordinates of *B* are **(9, –6)**.

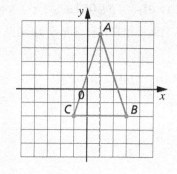

Translating 2D Shapes

- Translation moves a 2D shape into a new position on a grid using given directions.
- The shape stays exactly the same and is not rotated or reflected.

Example

The triangle *ABC* is translated by four squares to the left and two squares down. Find the new co-ordinates of *C*.

Mark vertex *C* with a dot. Count four squares left and then two squares down using the dot as a marker.

The new co-ordinates of *C* are **(4, 1)**.

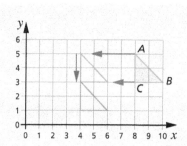

Problem Solving

- You will need to understand different types of direction to work out puzzles involving maps or moving objects through a maze.

> **Remember**
>
> Think about which direction the object is facing after each movement.

Example

A ladybird bot is in an enclosed maze. Find which instruction set will take it to the leaf.

(forwards = fd, backwards = bk, right = rt, left = lt)

A bk 1, lt 90°, fd 1, rt 90°, fd 3

B fd 5, rt 90°, fd 1

C bk 1, rt 90°, fd 4, lt 90°, fd 1

D fd 5, lt 90°, bk 1, lt 90°, fd 2, lt 90°, fd 2

E fd 3, rt 270°, fd 1, rt 90°, fd 2

Option **E** will take it to the leaf.

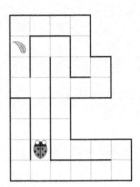

- A clock face is split into 12 equal sectors; each one is a 30° turn. The minute hand moves 30° every five minutes.
- To find the angles between clock hands, remember that the hour hand moves constantly too. Every hour that passes, the hour hand moves 30° around the clock face.

> **Remember**
>
> In 15 minutes, the minute hand will turn 90°.

Example

A clock shows the time is ten to twelve. What is the size of the angle made by the hands of the clock at this time?

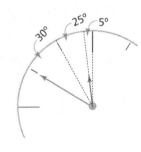

There are 90° between 9 and 12. So each step, say between 10 and 11, is 30°.

The hour hand is $\frac{5}{6}$ of the way between 11 and 12.

The 10 minutes for the hour hand is $\frac{1}{6}$ of 30° = 5°.

The angle between the two hands is 30° + 25° = **55°**.

> **Quick Test**
>
> 1. How many lines of symmetry does a regular pentagon have?
> 2. Shown on the right is a net diagram of a cube. How many edges of the cube appear twice in the net diagram?
>   A 4   B 5   C 6   D 7   E 8
> 3. The diagram (far right) shows a kite. Find the size of the angle marked *x*.
> 4. A fourth point *D* is added to the diagram (below right) so that *ABCD* form a square. What are the co-ordinates of *D*?
> 5. The end points of five lines are given below. Which pair of points forms a line parallel to the one shown in the diagram (right)?
>   A (–2, 1) and (2, –1)
>   B (–5, 1) and (4, 4)
>   C (–4, 0) and (2, 3)
>   D (–2, 0) and (3, 0)
>   E (2, 2) and (5, 3)

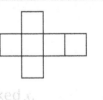

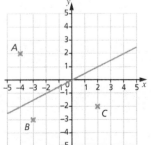

Statistics

You should be able to:

- read information from a range of statistical charts and graphs
- use the information given to find missing values or carry out calculations
- work out the average from a set of data.

Two-way Tables

- A two-way table shows information that relates to two different categories. You should be able to understand the information shown and be able to work out any missing values.

Example

Ashish's mum is placing an order for his school photo. There are four different photo packs available and she has started completing the order form:

	Price	Quantity	Total
Pack 1	£6.00		
Pack 2	£8.50	0	£0
Pack 3	£13.50	1	£13.50
Pack 4	£18.50	1	£18.50
		Postage	£1.75
		Total	£51.75

Ashish's mum still needs to fill in the row for Pack 1 but she will spend a total of £51.75, including £1.75 postage. How many lots of Pack 1 is Ashish's mum ordering?

First work out the cost of the packs ordered so far, plus the postage:

£13.50 + £18.50 + £1.75 = £33.75

Subtract this cost from the total: £51.75 – £33.75 = £18.00

The cost of each Pack 1 ordered is £6.00, so: £18.00 ÷ 6 = 3

She must be ordering **3** lots of Pack 1.

Distance Charts

- These charts show the distance between any places on the chart. To find a distance, read down from one place and across to the other.

Example

Look at this distance chart. How far is it from Longwell to Streetbridge?

Teeford				
390 km	Longwell			
245 km	296 km	Redham		
147 km	140 km	170 km	Streetbridge	
331 km	121 km	113 km	31 km	Octon

Follow the Longwell column down until you reach the Streetbridge row. The answer is **140 km**.

Pictograms

- Pictograms use small pictures or symbols to show amounts.
- Make sure you check what each small picture or symbol represents.

Example

This pictogram shows the number of children from classes who chose different fruit for their snack on Tuesday.
How many children were there altogether?

Multiply the whole fruits by the number they represent, then work out the proportions of the fractions to complete the calculations for each row.

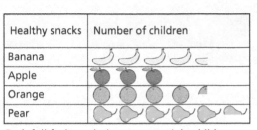

Healthy snacks	Number of children
Banana	
Apple	
Orange	
Pear	

Each full fruit symbol represents eight children

Bananas: $(4 \times 8) + (\frac{1}{2} \times 8) = 32 + 4 = 36$

Apples: $3 \times 8 = 24$

Oranges: $(4 \times 8) + (\frac{1}{4} \times 8) = 32 + 2 = 34$

Pears: $(5 \times 8) + (\frac{1}{2} \times 8) = 40 + 4 = 44$

Add up the totals: $36 + 24 + 34 + 44 = $ **138** children altogether

Bar Charts

- Bar charts compare frequencies (how many of one thing there are compared to another).

Example

Look at this bar chart, which shows how a class of pupils travel to school.
How many more children travel to school by car than by bicycle?

Read the values on the bar chart:

15 pupils travel by car and 5 pupils by bicycle.

So $15 - 5 = $ **10** more pupils travel to school by car than by bicycle.

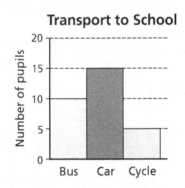

Transport to School

Line Graphs

- Line graphs can represent two different types of information: time-based data and conversion data.
- Time-based graphs show what happens to a measurement over time. It is important to check the time units when answering questions.
- The steepness of the line graph represents the rate of the change; a steep line shows a greater rate of change than a less steep line.

Example

Look at this line graph showing hours of sunshine in a village over the course of one week. How many days had 7 hours or more of sunshine?

For each day of the week, read straight up from the horizontal axis until you reach the line. Then read across to find the number of hours of sunshine for that day:

Monday: 5 hours of sunshine; Tuesday: 6 hours; Wednesday: 5 hours; Thursday: 7 hours; Friday: 8 hours; Saturday: 8 hours; Sunday: 6 hours

So **three** days of the week (Thursday, Friday and Saturday) had 7 hours or more of sunshine.

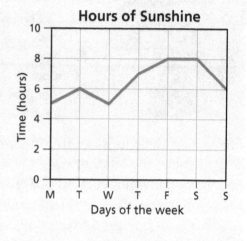

- Conversion graphs show relationships between amounts and how they compare in proportion. It is important to check the scale on both the *x*-axis and the *y*-axis.

Example

Look at the conversion graph.
How many euros would you get for £15?

The vertical axis doesn't reach as far as £15, but the constant steepness of the line shows that the rate of change is the same for all values.

If we find out how many euros £5 would be worth, we can multiply that value by 3 to get the conversion for £15.

From the vertical axis, read straight across until you reach the line of the graph. At that point, read directly down to find the equivalent value in euros.

The graph shows that £5 is equivalent to 6 euros.

6 × 3 = 18, so £15 is worth **18** euros.

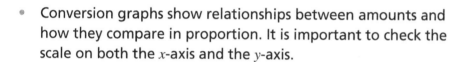

> **Remember**
>
> Harder questions may show line graphs which are curved rather than straight and/or they may ask you to find the difference between two different points on the line.

Pie Charts

- Pie charts are used to show fractions of a whole.
- The size of each segment of the circle represents the fraction of the whole.

Example

The pie chart below shows the hair colour of a group of parents. There are 16 parents in the group.

How many parents have the most common hair colour?

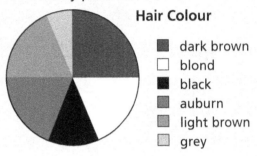

Hair Colour

- ■ dark brown
- ☐ blond
- ■ black
- ■ auburn
- ■ light brown
- ■ grey

> **Remember**
>
> When comparing information presented in differing forms, check scales and compare each item of information to identify any obvious errors or incorrect numbers. Graphs where measurements are given in different units are easy to misread.

To answer questions like this it is important to:

- make the link between the degrees at the centre of a circle when working out proportions
- find the number the pie represents.

Dark brown is the most common hair colour in this group and the dark brown segment represents $\frac{1}{4}$ of the parents. If there are 16 parents in total, then **four** of them have dark brown hair.

Venn Diagrams

- Venn diagrams show the relationships between data.
- Each circle represents a particular piece of information.
- Overlapping circles show where two more pieces of information share a common feature.

Example

Look at the Venn diagram shown (right).

Find the shape that fits into the section labelled 'x' in the diagram.

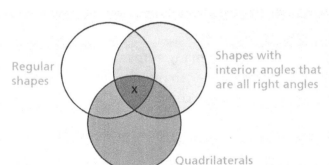

The answer is **B** because it is the only shape that shares all three properties: it is a regular quadrilateral with interior angles that are right angles.

Sorting Diagrams

- Sorting diagrams are used to sort objects or numbers into a grid – similar to a two-way table – depending on their properties.

Example

Look at this sorting diagram for numbers up to 30. It is not fully completed.

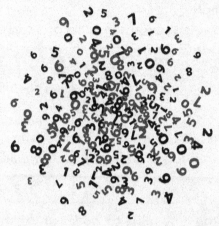

	Even numbers	Odd numbers
Prime numbers	2	3 5 7 11 13 17 19 23 29
Square numbers	?	1 9 25

Find a number which could be placed in the part of the diagram marked '?'

A 27   B 10   C 12   D 16   E 28

The answer must be both an even number and a square number. We can therefore rule out option A straight away, since it is an odd number. All the other options are even numbers but only one is a square number, i.e. 16. So the correct answer is **D**.

Average (Mean)

- The average, or the mean, is the sum of all the values divided by the number of values.
- So the mean of the numbers 2, 4, 4, 4, 5, 5, 6, 7, 8 is:

$$\frac{2 + 4 + 4 + 4 + 5 + 5 + 6 + 7 + 8}{9}$$

$$= \frac{45}{9} = 5$$

> **Remember**
>
> The mean can also be a fraction. If the number of children in five houses is 0, 1, 2, 2, 3, then the mean number of children per house is: $\frac{0 + 1 + 2 + 2 + 3}{5} = 1.6$ (even though you cannot have 0.6 of a child for real!)

Example

Romesh bought some apples while shopping at a supermarket. He bought two packs of six apples which each cost £1.20. He also bought three single apples which cost 30p each. What was the average cost of each apple that Romesh bought?

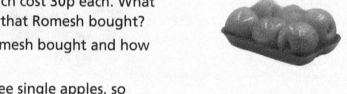

First work out how many apples Romesh bought and how much he spent in total on them:

He bought two packs of six and three single apples, so 6 + 6 + 3 = 15 apples in total

Two packs at a price of £1.20 each: 2 × £1.20 = £2.40

Three single apples at a price of 30p each: 3 × £0.30 = £0.90

Total spent on apples: £2.40 + £0.90 = £3.30 (or 330p)

To work out the average cost, divide the total cost by the number of apples bought:

330 ÷ 15 = **22p** per apple

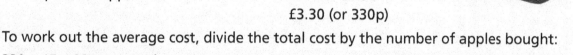

Averages from Frequency Tables

- Frequency tables often cause confusion. You need to remember that the frequency tells you how many numbers or data items there are altogether.

Example

This table shows the results of a survey of shoe sizes among children at a tennis club:

Shoe size	1	2	3	4	5
Frequency	2	1	6	1	2

What is the average shoe size among these children?
Write out the frequency line again, splitting this into the number of children with each shoe size.
The frequency total is 12, so there are 12 children.

Frequency	1, 1	2	3, 3, 3, 3, 3, 3	4	5, 5

Use the new table to work out the mean:

$1 + 1 + 2 + 3 + 3 + 3 + 3 + 3 + 3 + 4 + 5 + 5 = 36$

$36 \div 12 = 3$

The average shoe size is **3**.

Quick Test

1. The pictogram shows the results of a survey of favourite arts subjects among a group of pupils. How many more pupils prefer art compared with drama?

Favourite Arts Subject

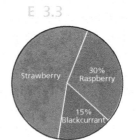

2. The line graph, shown far right, converts kilograms to pounds.
   How many pounds is 1.5 kg?
   A 0.6   B 0.7   C 1.1   D 2.2   E 3.3

3. This pie chart shows the percentages of different kinds of jam sold in a supermarket in one week.
   If the supermarket sold 45 jars of blackcurrant jam, how many jars of strawberry jam were sold?

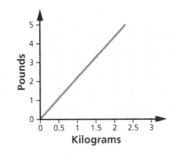

4. The table below shows the number of merit points scored in a class during the 12 weeks of term. The number of merit points for week 12 is missing.

Week	1	2	3	4	5	6	7	8	9	10	11	12
Merit points	6	5	6	8	10	7	6	7	10	3	10	?

If the mean number of merit points across the whole term was 7, how many merit points were scored in week 12?

Collins

11+
Maths
Practice & Assessment

1 What is the value of the '2' in this number?

6523

A 2 thousands   B 2 hundreds   C 2 tens   D 2 ones   E 2 tenths

2 What is this number in figures?

Two thousand, seven hundred and seven

A 2770   B 2707   C 207   D 2070   E 2007

3 Change the order of the digits in 5147 to make the smallest number possible.

A 1475   B 1754   C 1457   D 4157   E 7541

4 Alan played a game of hoopla at the school fair. If he managed to throw a hoop around any number less than −5, he would win a prize. Look at the hoops he ringed.

Hoops ringed: −7 −2 −5 −1 −4 −3 −8 −3 0 −6

How many prizes did Alan win?

A 2   B 3   C 4   D 5   E 6

5 Which letter is pointing at 1125?

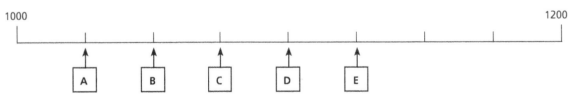

A A   B B   C C   D D   E E

6 Freddie is aged between 11 and 15. He counts on in steps of 7 from his age. He reaches the number 33.

How old is Freddie?

A 12   B 11   C 15   D 13   E 14

7 Which of these is the biggest number?

A 0.54   B 1.76   C 10.21   D 15.02   E 7.99

8 Look at the number line.

4.30   4.50

What number is the arrow pointing to?

A 4.34   B 4.36   C 4.38   D 4.40   E 4.42

9 What is 2135 rounded to the nearest ten?

A 2140   B 2150   C 2100   D 2130   E 2200

10 Look at the crowd attendance figures of the football clubs:

Round the attendance figures to the nearest 1000.

Which club rounds to a different value than the others?

Football Club	Attendance
Brunton Rovers	25 428
Hardside City	24 390
Newley Athletic	25 120
Oldfield Utd	24 818
Wilton Town	25 246

A Brunton Rovers   B Hardside City   C Newley Athletic   D Oldfield Utd   E Wilton Town

11 What is 20.394 correct to 1 decimal place?

A 20.3   B 20.4   C 21.0   D 20.0   E 20.5

12 Look at this list of temperatures:

19°C   −4°C   1°C   7°C   −10°C

Put the temperatures in order, starting with the warmest.

A 1°C   −4°C   7°C   −10°C   19°C
B 19°C   −10°C   7°C   −4°C   1°C
C 1°C   7°C   19°C   −10°C   −4°C
D 19°C   7°C   1°C   −4°C   −10°C
E −10°C   −4°C   1°C   7°C   19°C

13 Look at the number cards:

| −10 | 0 | −5 | −8 | 17 | −11 |

Which number lies halfway between the smallest number and the greatest number?

A 3   B 2   C 1   D 0   E −1

END OF TEST

1. Which pair of numbers would make this statement true?

   $$\boxed{} - \boxed{} = 10$$

   A 7, 3   **B** −5, −5   **C** 6, −4   **D** −8, −2   **E** 9, 1

2. Share 400 beads into eight equal groups. How many are in each group?

   A 40   **B** 50   **C** 60   **D** 45   **E** 80

3. Put the correct number in the box.

   $$23 \times 57 = 1300 + \boxed{}$$

   A 11   **B** 21   **C** 111   **D** 121   **E** 310

4. A famous mathematician claimed that every even number greater than 4 can be written as the sum of a pair of prime numbers.

   For example: 6 can be written as 3 + 3   8 can be written as 3 + 5

   Find a pair of prime numbers that sums to 18.

   A 13 and 7   **B** 16 and 2   **C** 9 and 9   **D** 11 and 7   **E** 15 and 3

5. Kia is trying to complete this subtraction but her calculator has two broken buttons, represented by $\boxed{}$ below.

   $$
   \begin{array}{r}
   5\ \ 6\ \ 5\ \ \boxed{} \\
   -\ \ 1\ \ 2\ \ \boxed{}\ \ 7 \\
   \hline
   \boxed{}\ \ 3\ \ 6\ \ 7
   \end{array}
   $$

   Which are the two broken buttons on her calculator?

   A 8 and 9   **B** 4 and 3   **C** 3 and 9   **D** 9 and 0   **E** 4 and 8

6. Five years ago, Ava celebrated her 18th birthday.

   How many years does Ava have to wait for her 30th birthday?

   A 12   **B** 5   **C** 8   **D** 9   **E** 7

7 Becky is multiplying a three-digit number by a two-digit number. She starts partitioning the numbers using the grid below but has not completed it.

×		30	4
50			
	600		24

What is the correct answer to Becky's multiplication?

A 5780   B 6700   C 7280   D 7474   E 7504

8 Castle High School is taking 37 pupils on a skiing trip. The flights cost £287 per person. The teachers go free.

What is the total cost of flights for the school?

A £8610   B £9184   C £10 045   D £10 619   E £11 193

9 What is the answer to this calculation?

$$5^2 - 4^3 =$$

A –2   B 39   C –33   D –39   E 13

10 There are 457 seats in the Grand Theatre.

If 23 minibuses with 15 people on them and five families with five people per family come to watch 'Guys and Dolls', how many spare seats will there be in the theatre?

A 87   B 112   C 345   D 432   E 25

11 Which of these sums gives the smallest answer?

A 12 × 11 + 14 – 13   B 11 × 12 + 13 – 14   C 13 × 14 + 12 – 11

D 14 × 12 + 13 – 11   E 12 × 13 + 11 – 14

12 At a golf club there are 1230 members.
- Men and children: 755 members
- Women and children: 700 members

How many children are members of the golf club?

A 530   B 55   C 230   D 225   E 475

13 Peter correctly did this calculation:

$$12 + 15 \div 3 + 6$$

What is the final answer?

| A 15 | B 23 | C 11 | D 3 | E 25 |

14 Thirty people go to a restaurant. All the diners choose from the Menu of the Day:

- Three courses for £12
- Two courses for £9

The total bill comes to £345. How many people had three courses?

| A 15 | B 18 | C 21 | D 23 | E 25 |

15 Clara makes 144 cup cakes for the school fair. It costs her 20p to make each cup cake, which she then sells at 70p each. All the cakes were sold.

How much profit did Clara make?

| A £100.80 | B £72 | C £50 | D £28.80 | E £12 |

16 Look at the cards below.

| $4^2 + \sqrt{16}$ | $3^2 + \sqrt{9}$ | $3^2 + 4^2$ | $5^2 - \sqrt{25}$ | $6^2 + 2^3$ |

Which two cards are equal in value?

A $4^2 + \sqrt{16}$ and $6^2 + 2^3$
B $5^2 - \sqrt{25}$ and $3^2 + 4^2$
C $3^2 + \sqrt{9}$ and $4^2 + \sqrt{16}$
D $3^2 + 4^2$ and $6^2 + 2^3$
E $4^2 + \sqrt{16}$ and $5^2 - \sqrt{25}$

17 Rapley High School has a total of 1862 staff and students.

| **Boys and staff total = 979** | **Girls and staff total = 1037** |

How many boys attend the school?

| A 825 | B 58 | C 883 | D 942 | E 963 |

18 There are 10 burgers in a box and 6 bread buns in a pack.

What is the least number of boxes of burgers and packs of bread buns you can buy, so that each burger has a bun, with nothing left over?

A 2 boxes of burgers and 3 packs of bread buns
B 3 boxes of burgers and 4 packs of bread buns
C 1 box of burgers and 2 packs of bread buns
D 3 boxes of burgers and 5 packs of bread buns
E 2 boxes of burgers and 2 packs of bread buns

19 Solve $(2.07 + 4 + 3.1 + 8.83) \div 3$

A 6   B 18   C 9   D 12   E 3

20 Look at this grid which has some empty spaces:

When every space is filled in, each row and column adds up to 23.

Which number should be in the space with the question mark?

7		8
	?	
3		9

A 2   B 3   C 4   D 5   E 6

21 Sunil thinks of a number between 1 and 20, including 1 and 20.

	Yes	No
Multiple of 4	✓	
Square number		✓
Factor of 24		✓

What is Sunil's number?

A 4   B 8   C 12   D 16   E 20

22 Asif is thinking of an odd number.

He adds another odd number to it and then multiplies the total by 4.

Which of these could be Asif's total?

A 225   B 230   C 233   D 240   E 249

END OF TEST

1 John scored 16 out of 48 in a maths test.

What is this as a fraction in its simplest form?

A $\frac{8}{24}$ B $\frac{4}{12}$ C $\frac{1}{2}$ D $\frac{1}{3}$ E $\frac{1}{4}$

2 Look at the diagrams.

$\frac{1}{4}$ of this shape is shaded:

What fraction of this shape is shaded?

A $\frac{1}{4}$ B $\frac{1}{8}$ C $\frac{1}{12}$ D $\frac{1}{16}$ E $\frac{1}{24}$

3 Look at the piece of ribbon.

In its simplest form, what fraction of the ribbon is green?

	300 mm		
blue	green	yellow	red
60 mm	8 cm	120 mm	4 cm

A $\frac{4}{15}$ B $\frac{3}{5}$ C $\frac{1}{2}$ D $\frac{1}{4}$ E $\frac{8}{30}$

4 All of the children had the same size bar of chocolate.

Bob ate $\frac{5}{6}$ of his bar, Suni ate $\frac{1}{4}$ of hers, Ahmed $\frac{3}{8}$ of his and Lisa $\frac{7}{12}$ of hers.

Put the fractions in order, starting with the largest amount of chocolate eaten.

A $\frac{7}{12}$ $\frac{3}{8}$ $\frac{1}{4}$ $\frac{5}{6}$ B $\frac{5}{6}$ $\frac{7}{12}$ $\frac{3}{8}$ $\frac{1}{4}$

C $\frac{1}{4}$ $\frac{3}{8}$ $\frac{5}{6}$ $\frac{7}{12}$ D $\frac{7}{12}$ $\frac{3}{8}$ $\frac{5}{6}$ $\frac{1}{4}$

E $\frac{5}{6}$ $\frac{3}{8}$ $\frac{7}{12}$ $\frac{1}{4}$

5 I am a fraction. I am equivalent to $\frac{60}{100}$. My numerator and denominator are both prime numbers.

Which fraction am I?

A $\frac{6}{10}$ B $\frac{30}{50}$ C $\frac{120}{200}$ D $\frac{3}{5}$ E $\frac{15}{25}$

6 Look at the diagrams.

Molly ate $\frac{1}{4}$ of the pepperoni pizza and $\frac{3}{8}$ of the chicken tikka pizza.

pepperoni pizza

chicken tikka pizza

What fraction of a whole pizza did she eat in total?

A $\frac{5}{8}$ B $\frac{3}{4}$ C $\frac{7}{8}$ D $\frac{2}{3}$ E $\frac{1}{2}$

7 Claire has £24 to spend. She spends $\frac{1}{6}$ of it on a book and $\frac{5}{8}$ of it on a new jumper.

How much money does Claire have left?

A £6   **B** £4   **C** £8   **D** £3   **E** £5

8 In a school $\frac{3}{7}$ of the pupils are boys. If there are 270 boys in the school, how many girls are there?

A 540   **B** 360   **C** 630   **D** 180   **E** 480

9 Abi has three bars of chocolate. She shares them equally between herself and four friends.

What percentage of one bar of chocolate do they each get?

A 25%   **B** 75%   **C** 20%   **D** 60%   **E** 80%

10 Wesley spent $\frac{2}{3}$ of his pocket money on sweets. He spent £2.70 on sweets.

How much pocket money did he have to begin with?

A £4.50   **B** £4.05   **C** £3.95   **D** £3.60   **E** £3.50

11 Izzie had some big buttons and some small buttons. She lined them up so that they measured the same distance.

If the diameter of the big button is 4.8 cm, what is the diameter of the small button?

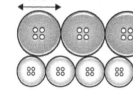
4.8 cm

A 2.4 cm   **B** 2.6 cm   **C** 3.6 cm   **D** 3.0 cm   **E** 3.2 cm

12 Use the number fact in the box to help you answer the question below.

What is 2.4 × 3.6?

$$24 \times 36 = 864$$

A 0.864   **B** 8.64   **C** 86.4   **D** 0.0864   **E** 0.00864

13 Look at the menu.

Troy ordered two portions of chips, a cola and three pizzas.
How much change did he get from a £20 note?

A £7.40   **B** £13.80   **C** £12.60   **D** £2.60   **E** £2.40

Menu

Chips	87p
Burger	£1.30
Cola	56p
Pizza	£1.70

14 A plank of wood measures 12.8 m. It is cut into pieces measuring 0.8 m.

How many pieces will the plank be cut into?

A 16   **B** 12   **C** 14   **D** 10   **E** 15

15 Put these decimals in descending order:

| 0.102 | 0.2011 | 0.003 | 0.1 | 0.0035 |

A	0.003	0.0035	0.1	0.102	0.2011
B	0.0035	0.2011	0.102	0.003	0.1
C	0.2011	0.102	0.1	0.003	0.0035
D	0.2011	0.102	0.1	0.0035	0.003
E	0.1	0.102	0.2011	0.003	0.0035

16 Look at the calculation in the box.

$$2.4 \times 0.3$$

What is the correct answer?

A 70.2 **B** 72 **C** 7.2 **D** 0.072 **E** 0.72

17 What fraction of the whole shape is shaded?

A $\frac{1}{2}$ **B** $\frac{1}{4}$ **C** $\frac{3}{10}$

D $\frac{1}{3}$ **E** $\frac{3}{8}$

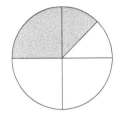

18 Look at the two statements.

| two rulers and three pencils cost £2.75 | two rulers and five pencils cost £3.45 |

Calculate the cost of one ruler.

A 85p **B** £1.70 **C** £1.05 **D** 35p **E** 70p

19 At a school fair you win a prize if you hit a prime number on this board with a dart.

2	3	18	4	9
33	15	6	17	14
13	27	23	16	8
29	8	30	1	11
34	12	5	26	22

What is the probability you will win a prize?

A 35% **B** 30% **C** 34% **D** 36% **E** 32%

20 Nadia has a box of pencils and pens. The table shows how many she has of each.

	Red	Blue	Green
Pencil	10	6	9
Pen	4	6	1

What is the probability that she randomly takes a red pen from the box?

A $\frac{1}{4}$ **B** $\frac{1}{6}$ **C** $\frac{1}{8}$ **D** $\frac{1}{9}$ **E** $\frac{1}{10}$

21 Look at the cards. There are two pairs of cards that sum to the same total, and an odd one out.

Which is the odd one out?

0.6	0.7	0.8	$\frac{3}{5}$	$\frac{7}{10}$
A	B	C	D	E

22 Billy went to a supermarket. There were five different coloured T-shirts in the sale. Each of them originally cost £12.

Which is the best buy?

Blue T-shirt $\frac{1}{3}$ OFF	Red T-shirt **25%** OFF	Green T-shirt $\frac{3}{4}$ OF THE ORIGINAL PRICE	YELLOW T-SHIRT REDUCED BY **20%**	Orange T-shirt PRICE SLASHED BY **£2**
A	B	C	D	E

23 This is a repeating pattern.

△△△ ☾☺☾♡ △△△ ☾☺☾♡

What fraction of the shapes are △?

A $\frac{6}{8}$ B $\frac{1}{3}$ C $\frac{3}{7}$ D $\frac{6}{15}$ E $\frac{2}{5}$

24 Dora had a glass of lemonade. She drank $\frac{1}{7}$ of it. There was 300 ml left in the glass.

How many millilitres were in the glass to begin with?

A 325 ml   B 350 ml   C 375 ml   D 400 ml   E 425 ml

25 5.03 + 0.066 = ?

A 5.69   B 5.96   C 5.366   D 5.069   E 5.096

26 Karly and Ahmed had the same history project to complete.

• Karly spent $\frac{5}{8}$ of a 24-hour day on hers.   • Ahmed spent $\frac{2}{3}$ of a 24-hour day on his.

Who spent more time on their project, and by how much?

A Karly, by 1 hour   B Ahmed, by 1 hour   C Karly, by 2 hours
D Ahmed, by 2 hours   E Ahmed, by 3 hours

27 Alan had a box of 80 chocolates. He ate 32 of them.

What percentage is left?

A 45%   B 60%   C 55%   D 50%   E 65%

END OF TEST

1. At Christmas, a chocolate manufacturer increased the size of their chocolate bar by 25%.

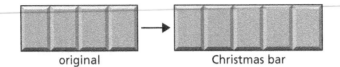

original   Christmas bar

After Christmas, the company decided to go back to the standard size.

What percentage did they remove to take it back to the original?

A 25%   B 10%   C 20%   D 15%   E 40%

2. Jonnie has 40 DVDs. Eighteen of these are comedy films.

What percentage are comedy films?

A 45%   B 40%   C 48%   D 30%   E 25%

3. In a box containing 300 apples, 15% of them are bad.

How many good apples are there?

A 250   B 200   C 285   D 45   E 255

4. At the school disco 48% of the pupils were girls.

If there were 24 girls at the disco, how many more boys than girls were there?

A 1   B 2   C 3   D 4   E 5

5. Tori's mum gives her £50 to save. She then gives her 5% of that original £50 every month to add to her savings.

How many months does it take Tori to save £70 in total?

A 2 months   B 4 months   C 6 months   D 8 months   E 10 months

6. Adam has a milk round. He gets paid £4.80 per hour. His boss decides to give him a 2.5% pay rise.

What is his new hourly rate of pay?

A £5.00   B £4.85   C £4.92   D £4.95   E £5.05

7 Look at the nutritional information for a 100 g serving of basmati rice.

Energy	120 kcal
Protein	2.6 g
Carbohydrate	26.0 g
Fat	0.2 g
Fibre	1.3 g

How many grams of carbohydrate would there be in 75 g of basmati rice?

A 18 grams **B** 22.5 grams **C** 19.5 grams **D** 2 grams **E** 32.5 grams

8 Shami makes a necklace. For every seven red beads there are four blue beads.

If there are 91 red beads, how many blue beads are there?

A 13 beads **B** 26 beads **C** 39 beads **D** 52 beads **E** 64 beads

9 Henry has 36 sweets. He decides to give them away, sharing them between Pavel and Orla in the ratio 2:7.

How many sweets does Orla get?

A 28 **B** 4 **C** 18 **D** 8 **E** 24

10 Orange squash is two parts juice to three parts water.

What fraction of the orange squash is juice?

A $\frac{2}{3}$ **B** $\frac{1}{2}$ **C** $\frac{1}{4}$ **D** $\frac{2}{5}$ **E** $\frac{3}{4}$

11 If 120 cm of ribbon costs 90p, how much would 2 m cost?

A £1.00 **B** £1.20 **C** £2.00 **D** £1.80 **E** £1.50

12 Two men took 6 days to build a wall. How long would it take three men to build the same wall?

A 4 days **B** 9 days **C** 12 days **D** 10 days **E** 8 days

13 Geeta makes 500 g of a snack mixture. 15% of the weight is peanuts, 30% is raisins and the rest is chocolate drops.

What is the ratio of raisins : chocolate drops : peanuts in its simplest form?

A 30:15:55 **B** 30:55:15 **C** 3:6:1.5 **D** 6:11:3 **E** 10:15:5

14 Look at the rectangle.

Each of the four sides is increased in length by 25%.

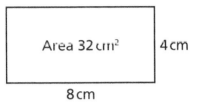

Area 32 cm²   4 cm

8 cm

What is the area of the new rectangle?

A 64 cm²   B 50 cm²   C 48 cm²   D 45 cm²   E 40 cm²

15 King Carlos had 3600 jewels to share between his two daughters, Princess Isabelle and Princess Julia, in the ratio 7:5.

How many jewels did Princess Isabelle get?

A 2100   B 1500   C 1800   D 2400   E 2000

16 One metre of ribbon is made up of red, white and blue.

Blue $\frac{1}{4}$ m	White 0.3 m	Red 45% of 1 m

What is the ratio of red : white : blue in its simplest form?

A $\frac{1}{4} : \frac{1}{3} : \frac{45}{100}$

B $0.25 : \frac{3}{10} : 45$

C $45 : 30 : 25$

D $0.25 : \frac{1}{3} : \frac{9}{20}$

E $9 : 6 : 5$

17 Craig has some cubes. They are all the same size. He makes a row of six cubes; it measures 144 cm.

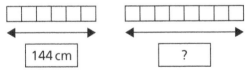

How long would a row of eight cubes be?

144 cm   ?

A 288 cm   B 192 cm   C 224 cm   D 176 cm   E 156 cm

18 Jodie had a party. For each person at the party, she had: four sandwiches, one packet of crisps, one can of cola and three hot dog sausages.

If there were 93 hot dog sausages, how many sandwiches did Jodie have at her party?

A 94   B 97   C 116   D 124   E 186

19 Organisers of a music festival are told they must have one security steward on duty for every 50 visitors. A crowd of 37 500 is expected to attend the festival.

How many security stewards must be on duty?

A 500 **B** 750 **C** 1000 **D** 800 **E** 200

20 A jumbo jet has a maximum cruising speed of 575 miles per hour.

How many miles will it travel in eight hours at maximum cruising speed?

A 4600 **B** 4150 **C** 2875 **D** 5175 **E** 3450

21 This graph shows the cost of a high-performance fuel at a petrol station.

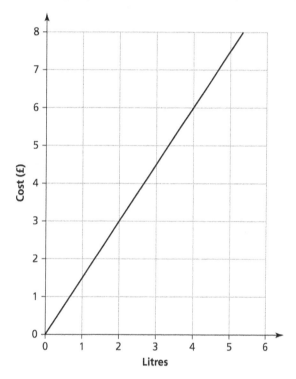

How much would 28 litres of this fuel cost?

A £28 **B** £32 **C** £42 **D** £35 **E** £45

END OF TEST

1 What is the next number in this sequence?

53	45	37	29	___

A 15 **B** 17 **C** 19 **D** 23 **E** 21

2 This sequence goes up in equal steps.

What is the third number in the sequence?

-7 ▢ **?** ▢ 5

A −4 **B** −3 **C** −2 **D** −1 **E** 0

3 $16 \times \triangle = 144$

$\triangle = ?$

A 6 **B** 7 **C** 8 **D** 9 **E** 10

4 $b - 15 = 9$

$b = ?$

A 6 **B** −6 **C** 24 **D** −24 **E** 25

5 $4d = 36$

$3d = ?$

A 27 **B** 28 **C** 25 **D** 24 **E** 18

6 Which sentence best describes the following sequence?

1   3   6   10   15   21

A The numbers increase by 2 each time.
B The previous number is multiplied by 3.
C They are cube numbers.
D The difference between each number increases by 1 each time.
E The previous number is multiplied by 2, then 1 is added.

7 The pattern below involves adding the same amount each time.

What is the third number in the sequence? -3 ▢ **?** ▢ 13

A 1 **B** 3 **C** 5 **D** 7 **E** 9

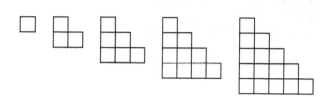

8 Look at this number pattern:

If you added the first and second term, second and third term, third and fourth term, etc., which sequence of numbers would be produced?

A Triangular   **B** Prime   **C** Cube   **D** Square   **E** Odd

9 x stands for a whole number.

| $x + 4$ is greater than 80 | | $x - 4$ is less than 80 |

Which numbers could x be?

A 75, 76, 77, 78, 79, 80, 81   **B** 76, 77, 78, 79, 80, 81, 82   **C** 77, 78, 79, 80, 81, 82, 83

D 78, 79, 80, 81, 82, 83, 84   **E** 79, 80, 81, 82, 83, 84, 85

10 Suri has four blocks that are the same weight.
Look at the equation:

What is the weight of each block?

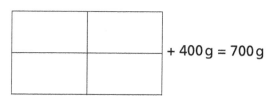

$+ 400\,g = 700\,g$

A 50 g   **B** 75 g   **C** 100 g   **D** 125 g   **E** 150 g

11 Read this information:

* Bill is y years old.
* Bill is 2 years older than Ben.
* Alvin is twice as old as Ben.

Which of these is an expression for Alvin's age?

A $2y - 4$ **B** $y + 2$ **C** $y - 2$ **D** $2y$ **E** $2y + 4$

12 This design has one large square and three identical smaller squares, with side length x cm.

How long is the side of the large square?

A 28 cm   **B** 20 cm   **C** 16 cm

D 18 cm   **E** 24 cm

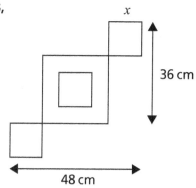

36 cm

48 cm

13 Look at this number machine.

NUMBER IN $\rightarrow$ +3 $\rightarrow$ ×4 $\rightarrow$ −1 $\rightarrow$ NUMBER OUT

If Nazneen got the number 27 out, what number did she put into the machine?

A 3 **B** 7 **C** 4 **D** 9 **E** 5

14 Miss Gilroy buys an empty pencil case for £5. Pens for the pencil case cost 32p each.

What expression would give the total amount that Miss Gilroy spends if she buys y pencils?

A $5y + 32$ **B** $32y + 5$ **C** $500y + 32$ **D** $5y + 0.32$ **E** $5 + 0.32y$

15 I use building blocks to create this pattern, which consists of five shapes.

 ? ?

How many building blocks do I need in total to create all five shapes in the pattern?

A 16 **B** 19 **C** 27 **D** 35 **E** 42

16 $2m + 17 = 20$

$m = ?$

A 3 **B** 2 **C** 0.5 **D** 1 **E** 1.5

17 Barry buys a pack of 30 non-rechargeable batteries.

His elder son, Josh, uses p batteries per week for playing on his games console.

His younger son, Lucas, doesn't play on his games console as much. He only uses q batteries per week.

After four weeks, there are just six batteries left in Barry's pack.

Which answer is correct?

A $p = 2$ and $q = 1$
B $p = 1$ and $q = 5$
C $p = 4$ and $q = 2$
D $p = 4$ and $q = 3$
E $p = 5$ and $q = 2$

18 Asad gets £6 pocket money a week. He saves it all because he wants to buy a mountain bike costing £637.

£6   £12   £18   £24   £30   …

Asad intends to buy the bike as soon as he has at least £637.

How much will he have left over after he has bought his new bike?

A £1   **B** £2   **C** £3   **D** £4   **E** £5

19 What is the formula for the perimeter of this isosceles triangle?

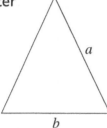

A $a + b$ **B** $2a + b$ **C** $a + 2b$ **D** $2a - b$ **E** $2a + 2b$

20 A snack bar offers these flavours of ice-slush drinks:

SLUSH Flavours	Strawberry
	Raspberry
	Orange
	Cherry
	Pineapple
	Bubble gum

Customers can buy a mixed slush which has any two different flavours from the choices above.

How many different choices of mixed slush does the snack bar offer?

A 15   **B** 12   **C** 10   **D** 24   **E** 18

21 Look at the spiral.

If you continued the spiral, which number would go in the shaded box?

A 86   **B** 76   **C** 78

D 72   **E** 82

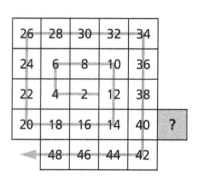

END OF TEST

1. Jack watched three television programmes from start to finish, which lasted a total of 2 hours 35 minutes.

   Which three programmes must he have watched?

The Sampsons	20 minutes
Mega Science	35 minutes
Newsday	15 minutes
Arctic Action	1 hour 55 minutes
Meerkat Mayhem	25 minutes

   A The Sampsons, Mega Science and Arctic Action
   B Mega Science, Newsday and Arctic Action
   C Newsday, Arctic Action and Meerkat Mayhem
   D Arctic Action, Meerkat Mayhem and The Sampsons
   E Meerkat Mayhem, The Sampsons and Mega Science

2. Peter wants to measure about 40 ml of liquid.

   What would be the best utensil for measuring this volume?

   A egg cup   B teaspoon   C large mug   D saucepan   E bucket

3. Fintan started Year 7 at 1.37 m tall. He ended Year 7 at 1.55 m tall.

   How many millimetres did Fintan grow over the year?

   A 180 mm   B 190 mm   C 200 mm   D 210 mm   E 220 mm

4. If November 25th is a Thursday, what day of the week will December 25th be?

   A Monday   B Wednesday   C Friday   D Saturday   E Sunday

5. Look at the weighing scale.

   Paula weighs some onions.

   If onions cost 60p per kilo, how much does Paula pay for her onions?

   A £1.68   B £1.80   C £1.92

   D £2.04   E £2.16

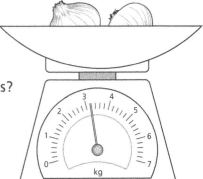

6 Japan is 9 hours ahead of London.

If it is 06.35 in Japan, what time is it in London?

A 15.35   B 03.35   C 18.35   D 21.35   E 09.25

7 Allie decided to go for a jog. She ran for 36.25 minutes.

How many seconds is this?

A 2160   B 2165   C 2185   D 2175   E 2180

8 The shape (right) was cut out of a piece of card measuring 14 cm by 10 cm.

What is the area of the card that has been discarded?

A 30 cm²   B 40 cm²   C 50 cm²

D 60 cm²   E 70 cm²

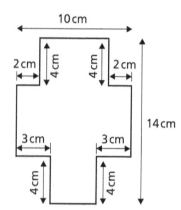

9 What is the perimeter of the shape shown in Question 8?

A 48 cm   B 50 cm   C 52 cm

D 54 cm   E 56 cm

10 Los Angeles is 8 hours behind London. A plane left London at 3.10pm and travelled for 11 hours and 5 minutes.

What was the time in Los Angeles when the plane arrived?

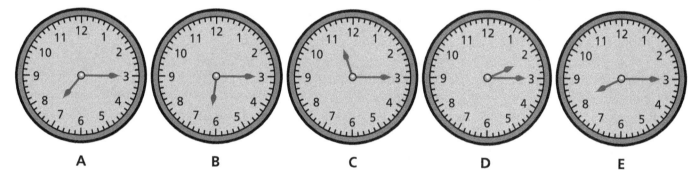

A   B   C   D   E

11 Look at the diagram of the bedroom.

By rounding the length of each wall to the nearest metre, estimate how many square metres of carpet would be needed to cover the whole room.

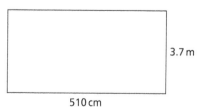

3.7 m

510 cm

A 20 m²   B 9 m²   C 18 m²   D 8 m²   E 15 m²

12 A small swimming pool is to be tiled. The bottom of the pool measures 6 m by 4 m. The two longer sides of the pool each measure 6 m by 2.5 m. The two shorter sides measure 4 m by 2.5 m.

A pack of tiles covers 30 m².

How many packs of tiles will the contractor need to supply to tile the pool?

A 1   **B** 2   **C** 3   **D** 4   **E** 5

13 Ariel's 30 cm ruler has shattered into pieces.

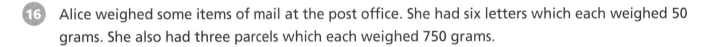

| 2 inches | 17 mm | 3 cm |

What size piece is still missing? Assume 1 inch = 2.5 cm

A 16.3 cm   **B** 17.3 cm   **C** 18.3 cm   **D** 19.3 cm   **E** 20.3 cm

14 A 3 kilowatt heater costs 60p per hour to run. It is left on from 3pm Monday until 6.30am the next day.

What is the cost of running the heater for that period?

A £1.98   **B** £16.50   **C** £7.75   **D** £9.30   **E** £5.00

15 Look at the box shown to the right.

Cubes measuring 20 mm by 20 mm by 20 mm are put in the box.

How many cubes can you fit into the box?

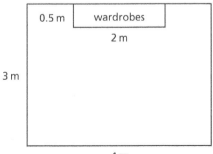

4 cm   8 cm   4 cm

A 20   **B** 16   **C** 8   **D** 4   **E** 12

16 Alice weighed some items of mail at the post office. She had six letters which each weighed 50 grams. She also had three parcels which each weighed 750 grams.

What was the total weight of Alice's mail?

A 2.25 kg   **B** 2.55 kg   **C** 1.8 kg   **D** 0.25 kg   **E** 25.5 kg

17 Lou decided to carpet her bedroom. She didn't need to carpet under the fitted wardrobes. The dimensions of the room are 4 m by 3 m. The dimensions of the fitted wardrobes are 2 m by 0.5 m.

How many square metres of carpet does Lou lay?

A 12 m²   **B** 14 m²   **C** 13 m²

D 10 m²   **E** 11 m²

0.5 m   wardrobes   2 m   3 m   4 m

18 A turkey takes 25 minutes per pound (lb) to cook plus an extra 25 minutes.

If Toni's turkey weighs 5 lbs, how long would she have to cook it for?

A 2 hours   **B** 2 hours 10 minutes   **C** 2 hours 20 minutes

D 2 hours 30 minutes   **E** 2 hours 40 minutes

19 Look at the diagrams. This rectangle and this square have the same perimeter.

8.2 cm   ?   15.8 cm

What is the area of the square?

A 144 cm²   **B** 36 cm²   **C** 64 cm²   **D** 100 cm²   **E** 121 cm²

20 Look at the diagram. The perimeter of the rectangle is 2 m.

What is the value of x?

x

62 cm

A 62 cm   **B** 38 cm   **C** 30 cm

D 26 cm   **E** 138 cm

21 The temperature reached 11°C on a winter's day, dropped by 19°C overnight and then increased by 5°C when the sun rose.

What was the temperature that morning?

A 1°C   **B** 3°C   **C** −8°C   **D** −5°C   **E** −3°C

22 This drinking glass holds 250 ml of water.

How many full glasses of water would be needed to fill the 2.25 litre jug?

A 9   **B** 8   **C** 10

D 11   **E** 5

2.25 litres

250 ml

23 A rectangular piece of card is cut so that its sides are whole centimetres and its area is 24 cm².

Which of these dimensions of rectangle could **not** have been cut?

A 12 cm × 2 cm   **B** 6 cm × 4 cm   **C** 7 cm × 5 cm   **D** 24 cm × 1 cm   **E** 8 cm × 3 cm

24 Suni had a £20 note. He bought five chews at 20p each and four chocolate bars at 42p each.

He shared the change between himself and three friends.

How much money did each of the four people each get?

| A £17.32 | B £5.77 | C £4.75 | D £4.58 | E £4.33 |

25 The volume of a cuboid is found by multiplying the three sides together.

If the volume is 1260 cm³, what is the missing length labelled x?

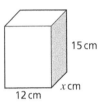

15 cm
x cm
12 cm

| A 5 cm | B 7 cm | C 15 cm | D 20 cm | E 10 cm |

26 Look at the parcel.

Bobby wrapped the parcel. He wanted to reinforce all the edges with packing tape.

What is the minimum length of packing tape he would need?

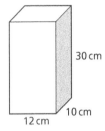

30 cm
10 cm
12 cm

| A 2.08 m | B 2.6 m | C 2 m | D 1.96 m | E 2.8 m |

27 Christian bought 54 ink cartridges at £12.75 each.

How much did he spend?

| A £68.85 | B £688.50 | C £6885 | D £6.88 | E £68 850 |

28 John and Paul go on a cycle ride. John rides for 2 hours at 16 km/h. Paul rides for 2 hours at 15 mph.

If 1 mile = 1.6 kilometres, which statement is true?

A John travels 2 km more than Paul.

B Paul travels 2 miles more than John.

C John travels 10 miles less than Paul.

D Paul travels 10 km more than John.

E They travel the same distance.

29 What is the volume of this chocolate bar in cm³?

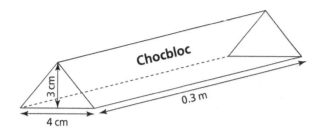

| A 360 cm³ | B 240 cm³ | C 300 cm³ | D 210 cm³ | E 180 cm³ |

30 The distance around the edge of this steam train wheel is 500 cm.

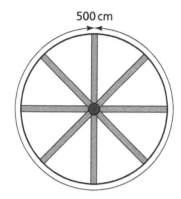

How many complete revolutions will the wheel make during a 12 km journey?

| A 1200 | B 6000 | C 2400 | D 3600 | E 4800 |

31 This fish tank has a capacity of 38 litres.

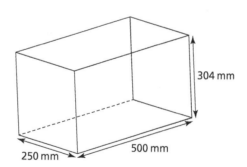

The owner will fill it so that the water will be 8 cm from the top of the tank.

How many litres of water will be in the tank?

| A 22 litres | B 25 litres | C 28 litres | D 30 litres | E 32 litres |

END OF TEST

1 Look at this map of a children's playground.

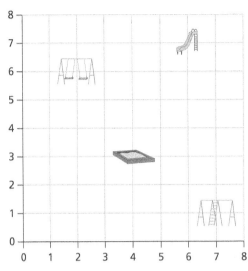

The swings are at (2, 6).

The slide is at (,   ).

A (7, 1) **B** (2, 6) **C** (4, 3) **D** (6, 7) **E** (7, 6)

2 Read these three clues:

| It has five faces. | It has eight edges. | It has five vertices. |

Which 3D shape do the clues describe?

A Square-based pyramid **B** Cuboid **C** Triangular-based pyramid

D Hexagonal prism **E** Triangular prism

3 Christian made this model out of straws. He uses one complete straw for each edge.

How many straws did Christian use to build the model?

A 14 **B** 17 **C** 16

D 15 **E** 18

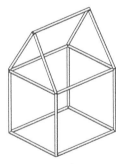

4 Look at the diagram.

What is the sum of the shaded angles at the bottom right of the triangle and the top right of the square?

A 140° **B** 170° **C** 130°

D 100° **E** 150°

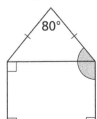

5 Eight identical parallelograms help to form a shape.

What is the size of the shaded reflex angle?

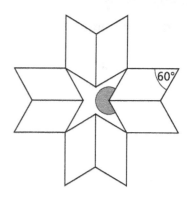

A 200°   B 300°   C 120°

D 60°   E 240°

6 Look at the grid.

A parallelogram has co-ordinates (4, 1), (2, 4), (−3, 4) and (?, ?).

What are the co-ordinates of the last point?

A (−3, 2)   B (−3, 1)   C (−1, 1)

D (4, 4)   E (2, −3)

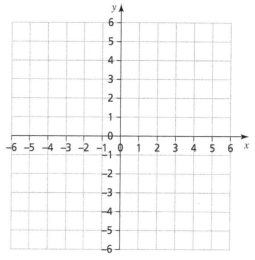

7 Look at the grid in Question 6. Louis plots two points on the grid, (3, −1) and (1, 2). He wants to draw an isosceles triangle.

Which one of the co-ordinates below can be a suitable third point?

A (5, −3)   B (1, −5)   C (−2, −1)   D (−1, −1)   E (3, 6)

8 The mouse is trying to get to the cheese. The shaded squares are mousetraps, so the mouse needs to avoid these squares. It starts off sitting facing to the left.

Which set of instructions should the mouse follow to get to the cheese?

Key: F = Forward, L = Left, R = Right

A F2, R90°, F4, L90°, F4

B F1, R90°, F3, L90°, F3, R90°, F1, L90°, F2

C F1, R90°, F2, L90°, F2, R90°, F2, L90°, F3

D F5, R90°, F2, L90°, F1, R90°, F2

E F4, R90°, F2, L90°, F2, R90°, F2

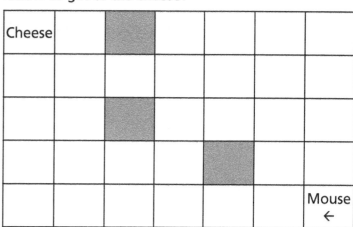

9 Look at this diagram.

Look at the line *PM* on the shape *MNOP*. What are the co-ordinates of the midpoint of this line?

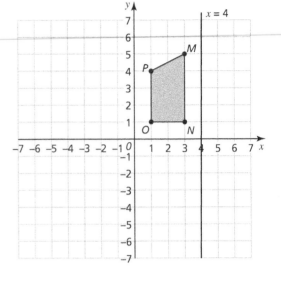

A (2, 4)

B (1, 4)

C (2, 5)

D (4.5, 2)

E (2, 4.5)

10 Look at the diagram in Question 9. Reflect the shape *MNOP* in the line $x = 4$.

What are the co-ordinates of vertex *O* in the reflected shape?

A (−1, 1)   **B** (1, −1)   **C** (6, 1)   **D** (−1, −1)   **E** (7, 1)

11 Look at the diagram in Question 9. Shape *MNOP* is translated four squares to the left and three squares down.

What are the co-ordinates of vertex *P* in the translated shape?

A (−3, 1)   **B** (−2, 0)   **C** (5, 1)   **D** (4, 0)   **E** (−3, 0)

12 Look at the diagram.

Find the value of x.

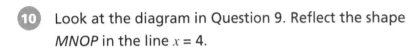

A 40°

B 15°

C 20°

D 30°

E 24°

13 The sum of the angles in a regular pentagon is 540°.

Look at the shape. Find the sizes of angle x and angle y.

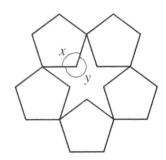

A $x = 90°$, $y = 270°$

B $x = 96°$, $y = 264°$

C $x = 100°$, $y = 260°$

D $x = 108°$, $y = 252°$

E $x = 124°$, $y = 236°$

14 Look at this diagram.

In the rectangle *ABCD*, *AB* is the length. The length is double the width.

What are the co-ordinates of the other two corners?

A (2, 5) and (–4, 5)
B (2, 4) and (–4, 4)
C (2, 3) and (–4, 3)
D (2, 1) and (–4, 1)
E (2, –5) and (–4, –5)

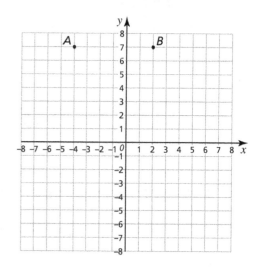

15 Look at the diagram in Question 14. Point *P* is (–5, –2) and point *Q* is (–1, 4).

What is the co-ordinate of the midpoint of *PQ*?

A (–2, 3)   B (–4, 0)   C (–3, –3)   D (–3, 1)   E (–3, 2)

16 Look at the diagram in Question 14. Point *X* is (4, –2) and point *Y* is (6, –5).

Which of these are the end points of a line that is parallel to *XY*?

A (2, –3) and (5, –3)   B (5, –1) and (7, –4)   C (5, –2) and (4, –5)

D (4, –3) and (6, –4)   E (3, –5) and (5, –7)

17 Samee is working out the angles between the hands of a clock. The clock shows four o'clock.

What is the smaller angle formed by the hands?

A 90°   B 100°   C 120°   D 150°   E 180°

18 This net is cut out of card. It is folded along the dashed lines.

Which shape will it make?

A Cuboid
B Triangular prism
C Triangular pyramid
D Square-based pyramid
E None of these

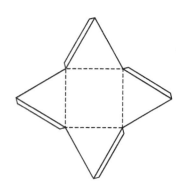

19 Olivia has drawn a rhombus.

Which property must the drawing have?

A   All angles are equal.

B   The shape has four lines of symmetry.

C   None of the sides are parallel.

D   All sides are equal in length.

E   Each of its four angles are different in size.

20 Which shape becomes a kite when reflected in the mirror line?

A 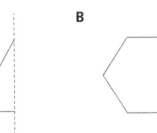   B 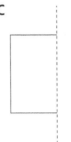   C   D   E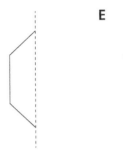

21 This is the rear view of a supermarket:

Which is the front view of the supermarket?

A 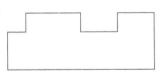   B    C

D    E

22 I am facing North-East and I can see a lake straight ahead. If I make a 180° turn, I can see a bridge.

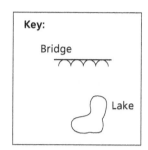

Which map correctly shows the position of the lake and the bridge?

A

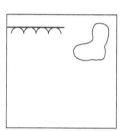

B

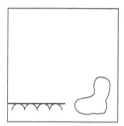

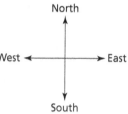

C

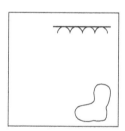

D

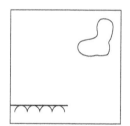

E

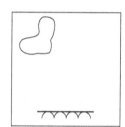

23 Which set of instructions will steer the car from the start (S) to the chequered flag (F), avoiding the oil patches? (F = forwards, L = left, R = right)

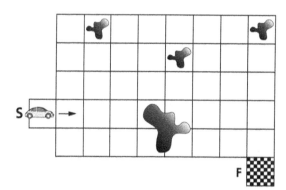

A F3, L, F3, R, F4, R, F4
B F3, L, F1, R, F5, R, F3
C F3, R, F1, L, F5, L, F1
D F3, L, F2, R, F5, R, F4
E F3, L, F1, R, F3, R, F2

END OF TEST

20 mins

1 This chart shows the distance in miles between different places.

Which pairs of places are the same distance apart?

Stockton				
98	Lancaster			
99	104	Sheffield		
14	87	98	Darlington	
67	94	35	62	Leeds

A   Leeds and Stockton AND Lancaster and Darlington

B   Lancaster and Sheffield AND Darlington and Leeds

C   Sheffield and Darlington AND Leeds and Stockton

D   Darlington and Leeds AND Stockton and Sheffield

E   Stockton and Lancaster AND Sheffield and Darlington

2 The table shows the results of a maths test.

Which of these statements is **not** true?

A   34% of pupils scored over 60 marks.

B   18 pupils scored 40 or less.

C   25 pupils scored between 21 and 60 marks.

D   The most common score was 41–60 marks.

E   Fewest pupils scored 0–20 marks.

Test result	Frequency
0–20 marks	8
21–40 marks	10
41–60 marks	15
61–80 marks	13
81–100 marks	4

3 This bar chart shows the month in which a group of students have their birthday.

How many students have their birthday in the first six months of the year?

A   27

B   31

C   30

D   28

E   29

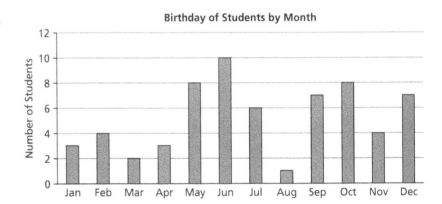

Birthday of Students by Month

4 A tennis club has 60 members.

How many girls at the club are 10–14 years old?

A   22   B   12   C   15

D   9   E   7

Age range	Boys	Girls	Total
Under 10		8	15
10–14 years			
Over 14	11		23
Total		27	60

5 Four children had their weight measured and the results are shown in the table.

What is the mean weight of the four children?

Child	Weight
Henry	32 kg
Sushila	29 kg
Olivia	28 kg
Waseem	35 kg

A 30 kg   **B** 31 kg   **C** 32 kg

D 33 kg   **E** 34 kg

6 Anji got some progress marks for different subjects on her school report.

The marks (which are out of 10) are shown in the table.

	Term 1		Term 2		Term 3	
	Start	End	Start	End	Start	End
Maths	1	3	3	4	4	5
English	2	4	4	6	6	7
Science	1	2	2	4	4	7
Music	1	3	3	5	5	6
Art	3	5	5	7	7	9
Spanish	2	5	5	6	6	8

In which subject did Anji make greatest progress between the start of Term 2 and the end of Term 3?

A Science   **B** Art   **C** Music   **D** English   **E** Spanish

7 This pie chart shows the results of a survey about people's favourite films.

If 36 people liked 'The Superheroes', how many people were surveyed altogether?

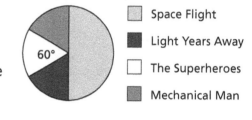

Space Flight
Light Years Away
The Superheroes
Mechanical Man

A 216   **B** 144   **C** 6   **D** 180   **E** 108

8 A survey was carried out at a cinema as to which type of film people liked to watch. This Venn diagram shows the results.

How many people liked to see science fiction and/or comedy films, but not romance?

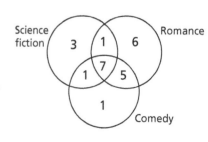

A 3   **B** 4   **C** 5

D 6   **E** 7

9 Look at the conversion graph.

Phil had a bag of potatoes weighing 5.5 kg.

How many pounds would this be to the nearest pound?

A 3

B 12

C 10

D 6

E 13

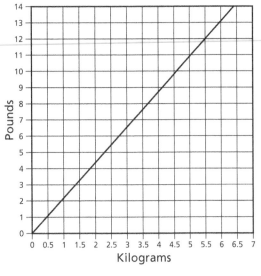

10 The pie chart represents 60 pupils. They were asked which flavour of crisps was their favourite.

Which of these statements about the pie chart is **not** true?

A One quarter of the pupils like chicken flavour.

B 50% of the pupils like ham or salt and vinegar.

C Less than 10% of the pupils like plain crisps.

D $\frac{1}{3}$ of the children like salt and vinegar flavour.

E $\frac{1}{6}$ of the children like prawn flavour.

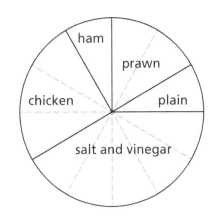

11 This pictogram shows how many bicycles were sold by a shop in one week. The shop is closed on Mondays.

Key: 🚲 = 4 bicycles sold

On how many days of the week did the shop sell more than 5 bicycles?

A 1
B 2
C 3
D 4
E 5

Monday	
Tuesday	🚲 🚲
Wednesday	🚲
Thursday	🚲
Friday	🚲 🚲
Saturday	🚲 🚲 🚲
Sunday	🚲 🚲

12 The 60 children who attended a multi-sports holiday club were surveyed to find out which activities they liked best. This chart shows the proportion of children who most liked each sport. There are no numbers along the *y*-axis.

Favourite Sports

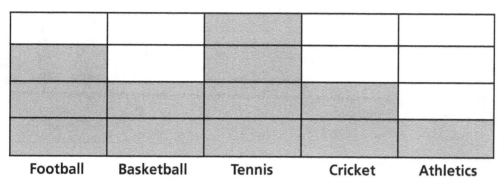

Which sport was the favourite of 15 children?

A Football   **B** Basketball   **C** Tennis   **D** Cricket   **E** Athletics

13 Look at this sorting diagram.

	At least one pair of parallel sides	No parallel sides
All angles are equal		
Angles are not all equal		

Which of these shapes could go in the shaded part of the diagram?

A Square   **B** Rectangle

C Equilateral triangle   **D** Rhombus

E Trapezium

14 The bar chart shows the favourite colour of 20 children.
The page folded over and some of the bar chart is missing.

How many children chose purple as their favourite colour?

A 8

B 9

C 10

D 11

E 12

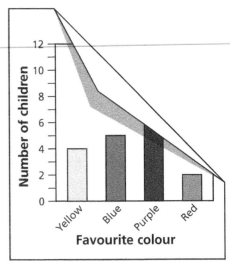

15 There is an ink blotch on Marni's French result. She knows that English was 40, Maths 56, German 70 and History 66, but she can't see the French mark. She knows the mean of the five exam results is 56 marks.

What was her French result?

A 52 marks   B 48 marks   C 50 marks   D 46 marks   E 54 marks

16 A Scout leader recorded the temperature every hour during a camping trip. The line graph shows the results.

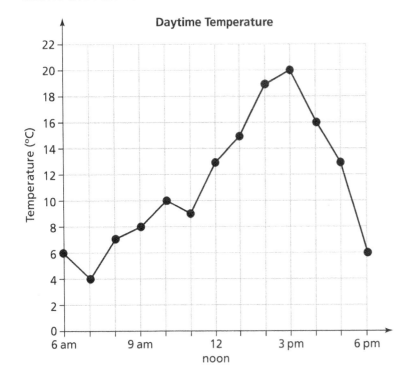

By how many degrees Celsius did the temperature change between 9 am and 3 pm?

A 10 degrees   B 12 degrees   C 8 degrees   D 14 degrees   E 15 degrees

17 What is the mean of these three expressions?

$5y + 3$ $7y + 4$ $3y - 1$

A $5y + 2$ **B** $4y + 3$ **C** $6y + 1$ **D** $4y + 1$ **E** $5y + 1$

18 This line graph shows how the volume of water in a storage tank decreased over a period of 12 days. The storage tank was full of water at the start of the 12-day period.

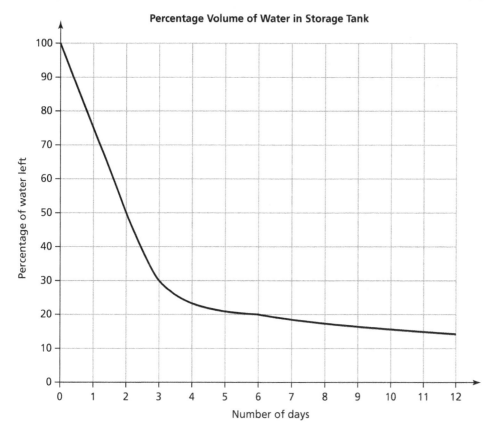

How many days did it take for the water in the tank to fall to $\frac{1}{5}$ of its original volume?

A 12   **B** 10   **C** 2   **D** 3   **E** 6

END OF TEST

THIS PAGE HAS DELIBERATELY
BEEN LEFT BLANK

Collins

Mathematics Multiple Choice Practice Paper 1

Read these instructions carefully:

1. You must not open or turn over this booklet until you are told to do so.

2. This booklet is a multiple-choice test containing different types of questions.

3. Do all rough working on a separate sheet of paper.

4. You should mark your answers in pencil on the answer sheet provided, not on this booklet.

5. Rub out any mistakes as well as you can and mark your new answer.

6. Try to do as many questions as you can. If you find that you cannot do a question, do not waste time on it but go on to the next one.

7. If you are stuck on a question, choose the answer that you think is best.

8. You have 50 minutes to complete the test.

1 What is the value of the 7 in this number?

32 750

A 7 ones **B** 7 tens **C** 7 hundreds **D** 7 thousands **E** 7 ten thousands

2 A 130 cm sheet of metal is cut into lengths of 40 cm.

What is the length of the metal sheet left over?

A 5 cm   **B** 10 cm   **C** 15 cm   **D** 20 cm   **E** 25 cm

3 An ice cream shop asks its customers their favourite flavour of ice cream.

 represents 20 people

How many more people said they like chocolate than said they like vanilla?

A 30 people   **B** 5 people   **C** 10 people

D 15 people   **E** 25 people

Flavour	Number of people
Chocolate	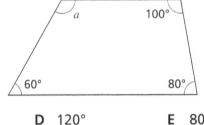
Vanilla	
Strawberry	

4 What is the size of the angle a in this trapezium?

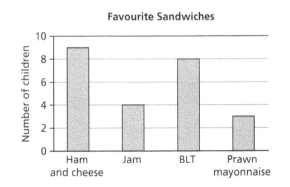

A 110°   **B** 100°   **C** 60°   **D** 120°   **E** 80°

5 Sharon asked her class about their favourite type of sandwich and displayed the results in a bar chart.

How many children preferred sandwiches other than jam?
(Ham and cheese, BLT and prawn mayonnaise)

A 12 children   **B** 14 children   **C** 4 children

D 24 children   **E** 20 children

Favourite Sandwiches

6 Aamirah records the height of her climbing bean plant.

One week her plant was 1.54 metres high. It grew
3 centimetres in the week.

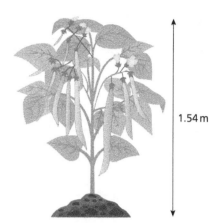

1.54 m

How many metres high was her plant then?

A 1.57 m **B** 15.43 m **C** 157 m **D** 0.157 m **E** 1.543 m

7 Here is a net of a 3D shape.

Which 3D shape can be made from this net?

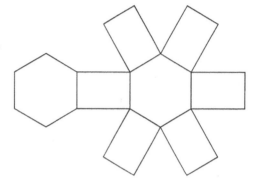

A Cuboid **B** Cube **C** Pentagonal prism **D** Hexagonal prism **E** Square-based pyramid

8 Mieke asked 120 Year 6 children about their favourite
type of book and displayed the results in a pie chart.

**How many children said their favourite type was a
fiction genre?**
(Adventure, science fiction or mystery)

Non-fiction

Science fiction

Adventure

Mystery

A 105 children **B** 100 children **C** 90 children **D** 80 children **E** 75 children

9 José pours sugar from a 1 kilogram bag into a storage
container that will hold 850 grams of sugar.

How much sugar is left in the bag?

A 1.5 kg **B** 15 g **C** 0.15 kg **D** 0.015 kg **E** 1.05 g

10 Here is a graph showing the weight of a duckling in the first 6 weeks.

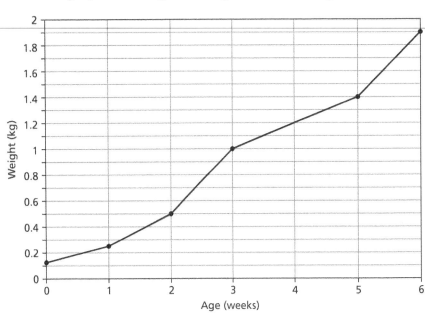

Approximately how much did the duckling weigh at 4 weeks?

A 1.02 kg   **B** 1.0 kg   **C** 1.4 kg   **D** 1.2 kg   **E** 1.1 kg

11 A shop is having a sale. Everything is 15% off. A pair of jeans originally cost £25.00.

How much do you save buying the jeans in the sale?

A £10.00   **B** £15.00   **C** £3.75   **D** £2.50   **E** £5.00

12 The time graph shows Ava's journey walking to school.

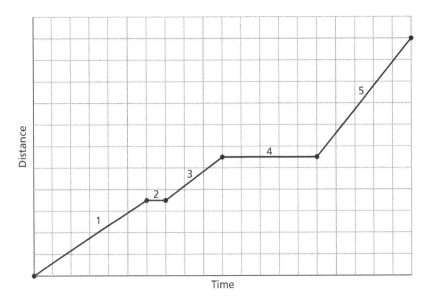

Which section of the graph shows the time period in which she was walking the fastest?

A Section 1   **B** Section 2   **C** Section 3   **D** Section 4   **E** Section 5

13 The cost of a taxi in pounds (C) is calculated using the formula $C = 5 + 2(x - 1)$ where x is the number of miles travelled.

How much does a 9-mile journey cost?

A £9.00   **B** £21.00   **C** £16.00   **D** £5.00   **E** £14.00

14 Here is a map of a village:

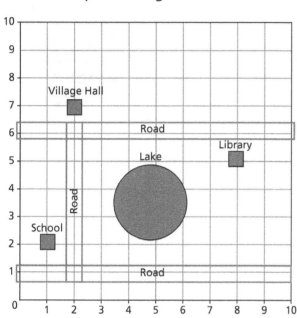

What are the co-ordinates of the village hall?

A (2, 1)   **B** (7, 2)   **C** (1, 2)   **D** (8, 5)   **E** (2, 7)

15 The parallelogram is reflected in the mirror line shown.

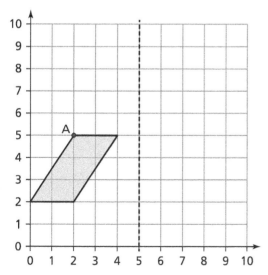

What are the co-ordinates of point A in the reflection?

A (5, 8)   **B** (5, 9)   **C** (8, 5)   **D** (7, 5)   **E** (8, 9)

16 The radius of a circle is 15 cm.

How far is the distance across the circle through the centre?

A 30 cm   B 25 cm   C 15 cm   D 20 cm   E 7.5 cm

17 Five classes take a times tables test. The scores are shown in this table.

Class	Score
Class 1	13
Class 2	17
Class 3	20
Class 4	14
Class 5	16

What is the mean score?

A 20   B 12   C 16   D 17   E 10

18 George is collecting trading cards. There are 84 to collect. He has $\frac{3}{4}$ of them.

How many trading cards does he have?

A 63   B 21   C 42   D 11   E 8

19 A bucket holds 1250 ml of water when full. Water is poured into the empty bucket from a jug holding 0.75 l of water.

One full jug of water is poured into the bucket.

How much more water can the bucket hold?

A 0.25 l   B 500 ml   C 450 ml   D 0.75 l   E 350 ml

20 What are the co-ordinates of the point X shown on the grid?

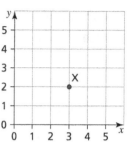

A (2, 2)　　　B (2, 3)　　　C (3, 3)　　　D (3, 2)　　　E (1, 2)

21 This bar chart shows some children's favourite sweets.

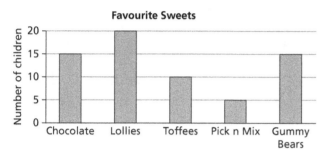

Which sweets did the most number of children say was their favourite?

A Pick n Mix　　B Chocolate　　C Toffees　　D Lollies　　E Gummy Bears

22 Order the fractions from smallest to largest.

$\frac{1}{2}$　　$\frac{3}{4}$　　$\frac{1}{8}$　　$\frac{5}{8}$　　$\frac{7}{8}$

A $\frac{1}{8}$　$\frac{5}{8}$　$\frac{1}{2}$　$\frac{3}{4}$　$\frac{7}{8}$

B $\frac{1}{8}$　$\frac{1}{2}$　$\frac{5}{8}$　$\frac{3}{4}$　$\frac{7}{8}$

C $\frac{1}{8}$　$\frac{3}{4}$　$\frac{5}{8}$　$\frac{1}{2}$　$\frac{7}{8}$

D $\frac{1}{8}$　$\frac{5}{8}$　$\frac{7}{8}$　$\frac{1}{2}$　$\frac{3}{4}$

E $\frac{1}{8}$　$\frac{7}{8}$　$\frac{3}{4}$　$\frac{1}{2}$　$\frac{5}{8}$

23 A train is due to arrive at a station at 11.15. It is 48 minutes late.

At what time did the train arrive?

A 12.03　　　B 11.15　　　C 11.48　　　D 12.00　　　E 12.48

24 Zainab is buying ribbon to place around the perimeter of a baby blanket. The blanket is 1 metre wide and 1.5 metres long.

What length of ribbon does she need?

A 7.5 m　　　B 7 m　　　C 2.5 m　　　D 5 m　　　E 3 m

25 The timetable for a train between London Bridge and Brighton is shown here. Amanda takes the train that leaves London Bridge at 16.51.

London Bridge	16.51	17.09	17.41
East Croydon	- - - - - -	17.26	- - - - - -
Gatwick Airport	17.21	17.42	- - - - - -
Preston Park	17.55	- - - - - -	18.48
Brighton	18.01	18.17	18.53

How long does it take her to get to Preston Park?

A 10 minutes **B** 54 minutes **C** 4 minutes **D** 70 minutes **E** 64 minutes

26 This chart shows some children's favourite vegetables.

How many children said 'green vegetables' were their favourite?
(broccoli, green beans and peas)

A 6 **B** 18 **C** 4 **D** 10 **E** 12

27 Here is a diagram showing even numbers and multiples of 3:

Which number could go in the shaded intersection of the diagram?

A 15 **B** 14 **C** 9 **D** 18 **E** 8

28 Kaya earns £1.50 pocket money each week. She is saving up to buy a toy that costs £18.00.

If she saves all the money she earns, how many weeks will it take her to save £18.00?

A 18 weeks **B** 12 weeks **C** 10 weeks **D** 15 weeks **E** 8 weeks

29 How many of the smaller squares can fit into the larger rectangle?

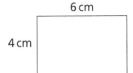

A 12 **B** 20 **C** 6 **D** 24 **E** 18

30 One day in June the temperature was 18.5°C. The next day was 2°C cooler.

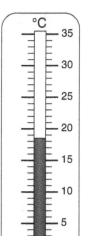

What temperature was it the next day?

A   18.5°C

B   20.5°C

C   18.3°C

D   18.8°C

E   16.5°C

31 Aisha is buying wood to make a rectangular picture frame. She wants the frame to be 75 cm wide and 40 cm tall.

How much wood does she need?

A   230 cm   B   115 cm   C   150 cm   D   200 cm   E   300 cm

32 This graph shows the world population over time.

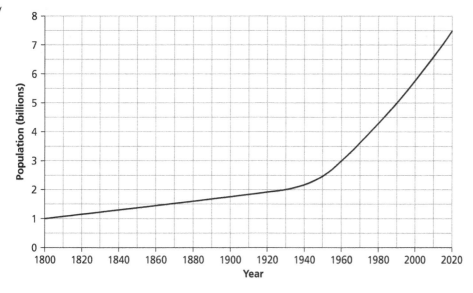

In which year was population half what it was in 1990?

A   1980   B   1960   C   1950   D 2000   E 1800

33 **What is the missing number?**

630 × 3 = 1890   630 × ☐ = 18.9

A   0.003   B   0.3   C   0.03   D   3   E   30

34 This bar chart shows the number of children who went to the playground after school each day.

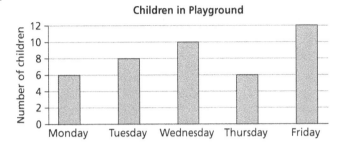

How many children went to the playground over the five days?

A 18 children   B 24 children   C 52 children   D 14 children   E 42 children

35 What is $\frac{15}{16} - \frac{3}{8}$?

A $\frac{9}{16}$ B $\frac{12}{8}$ C $\frac{8}{12}$ D $\frac{1}{8}$ E $\frac{16}{9}$

36 The length of each side of this cube was tripled.

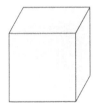

How much did the volume increase by?

A 27 times   B 9 times   C 18 times   D 2 times   E 12 times

37 Harper ran a race for charity. She raised £2.50 for every 100 metres she ran.

How much did she raise for the charity if she ran 1500 metres?

A £15.50   B £375.00   C £250.00   D £25.00   E £37.50

38 An angle is shown (right).

Which statement is incorrect?

A The angle is more than 90 degrees.
B The angle is less than 90 degrees.
C The angle is less than 360 degrees.
D The angle is more than 180 degrees.
E The angle is more than 45 degrees.

39 Rebecca wins £360 in a prize draw. She decides to share this equally with her two sisters.

Share £360 into three equal parts.

A £40   B £60   C £120   D £80   E £50

40 A ladybird travels 562 metres in one day.

How many metres does the ladybird travel in one week?

A 1124 m　　**B** 3934 m　　**C** 3967 m　　**D** 3423 m　　**E** 1524 m

41 Here is a pentagon.

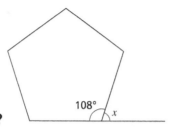

What is the size of angle x?

A 108°　　**B** 82°　　**C** 90°　　**D** 72°　　**E** 180°

42 Here is a bar chart showing the number of children who prefer different seasons. The y-axis does not have a scale shown. 140 children were surveyed.

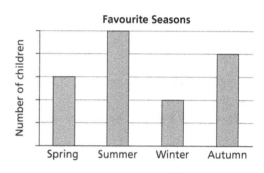

How many children prefer summer?

A 5　　**B** 50　　**C** 10　　**D** 100　　**E** 60

43 Here is a box and its net.

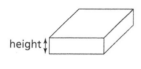
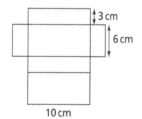

What is the height of the box?

A 16 cm　　**B** 6 cm　　**C** 10 cm　　**D** 9 cm　　**E** 3 cm

44 **What percentage of £20 is 20p?**

A 10%　　**B** 0.1%　　**C** 1%　　**D** 0.01%　　**E** 100%

45 Evelyn drives 120 miles from London to Bristol. It takes her 3 hours.

What is her average speed in miles per hour?

A 100 mph　　**B** 60 mph　　**C** 70 mph　　**D** 40 mph　　**E** 50 mph

46 Which of the following transformations is a reflection?

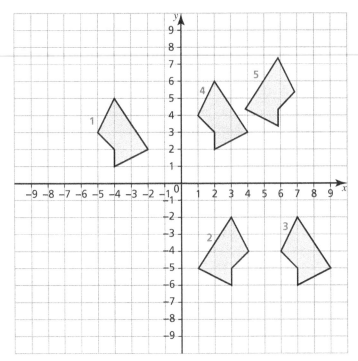

A Shape 2 to Shape 5

B Shape 1 to Shape 4

C Shape 4 to Shape 3

D Shape 3 to Shape 1

E Shape 2 to Shape 3

47 What is the missing number in this calculation?

180 ÷ ☐ = 15

A 10   B 24   C 6   D 12   E 15

48 A bus leaves Madrid at 10.50. It arrives in Toledo at 12.14.

How many minutes did the journey take?

A 64 minutes   B 74 minutes   C 84 minutes   D 24 minutes   E 36 minutes

49 Maisy records the number of times tables questions she completes correctly in one minute.

After four tests, her mean number correct is 20 questions.

After five tests, her mean number correct is 21 questions.

How many questions did she get correct on the fifth test?

A 25   B 20   C 18   D 21   E 15

50 The co-ordinates of the three vertices of a shape are:

(x, y) $(x - 3, y - 4)$ $(x + 3, y - 4)$

What shape is this?

A Rectangle   B Isosceles triangle   C Scalene triangle   D Kite   E Pentagon

END OF PAPER

Collins

Mathematics Multiple Choice Practice Paper 2

Read these instructions carefully:

1. You must not open or turn over this booklet until you are told to do so.

2. This booklet is a multiple-choice test containing different types of questions.

3. Do all rough working on a separate sheet of paper.

4. You should mark your answers in pencil on the answer sheet provided, not on this booklet.

5. Rub out any mistakes as well as you can and mark your new answer.

6. Try to do as many questions as you can. If you find that you cannot do a question, do not waste time on it but go on to the next one.

7. If you are stuck on a question, choose the answer that you think is best.

8. You have 50 minutes to complete the test.

1

What number does the arrow point to on this number line?

A 12.4   **B** 12.5   **C** 12.2   **D** 12.25   **E** 12.35

2

One day in December the temperature was 7.5°C. The next day it was 3 degrees warmer.

What temperature was it the next day?

A 4.5°C   **B** 7.8°C   **C** 10.5°C

D 7.2°C   **E** 10.8°C

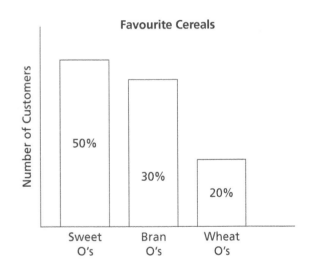

3

Choose the option that shows this number in figures:

seven thousand and ninety-five

A 7095   **B** 7905   **C** 7950   **D** 70 905   **E** 70 950

4

Bran O's asked customers going into a shop about which brand of cereal they preferred. They presented their data in this misleading bar chart.

What makes the chart misleading?

A The bars are not evenly spaced.
B The height of the bars is not to scale.
C Wheat O's is lower than Bran O's.
D There is no scale on the x-axis.
E Sweet O's is higher than Bran O's.

Favourite Cereals

5

Here are five shapes:

   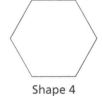 

Shape 1   Shape 2   Shape 3   Shape 4   Shape 5

Which shape is a regular pentagon?

A Shape 1   **B** Shape 2   **C** Shape 3   **D** Shape 4   **E** Shape 5

6 Amelia is training to run a 5 km race. She records her time each day.

Day	Saturday	Sunday	Monday	Tuesday	Wednesday
Race time	50 mins	45 mins	45 mins	42 mins	43 mins

What is her mean race time?

A 50 minutes   **B** 47 minutes   **C** 43 minutes   **D** 45 minutes   **E** 48 minutes

7 Kieran is twice as old as Lilly. In three years he will be 13.

How old is Lilly?

A 13   **B** 8   **C** 10   **D** 20   **E** 5

8 Inga drives to work. Her journey lasts three-quarters of an hour. She arrives at work at 8.50 am.

At what time did she leave home?

A 8.45 am   **B** 8.15 am   **C** 8.05 am   **D** 9.30 am   **E** 9.45 am

9 Nyah is buying squash for a party. Each bottle has 30 servings of 50 ml each.

How many litres are in the bottle?

A 1.5 litres   **B** 500 litres   **C** 15 litres   **D** 1500 litres   **E** 0.015 litres

10 Here is an equilateral triangle.

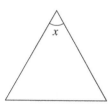

What is the size of angle x?

A 180°   **B** 120°   **C** 60°   **D** 45°   **E** 90°

11 **What is the missing term in this sequence?**

−11   −6   −1   ☐

A −4   **B** 4   **C** 1   **D** −6   **E** 0

12 This bar chart shows the number of children who voted for each candidate for Head Girl.

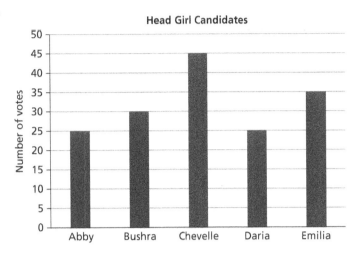

Which candidate received the most votes?

A Abby   **B** Bushra   **C** Chevelle   **D** Daria   **E** Emilia

13 Here is a graph to convert between litres and pints.

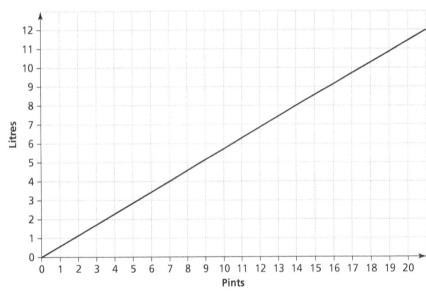

Approximately how many litres is 7 pints?

A 4 litres   **B** 8 litres   **C** 10 litres   **D** 7 litres   **E** 5 litres

14 Which number completes this calculation?

$56 \times 99 = 5600 - \boxed{}$

A 10   **B** 560   **C** 650   **D** 100   **E** 56

15 Some children were asked their favourite colours.
Their responses are shown here.

	● 10 children
Purple	● ● ● ◖
Red	● ● ●
Green	● ●
Blue	● ● ● ● ●
Orange	● ◖
Pink	● ● ◖

How many children were surveyed?

A 18 children   **B** 21 children   **C** 100 children

D 175 children   **E** 125 children

16 **What is the missing number in this calculation?**

9 × ☐ = 162

A 15   **B** 9   **C** 81   **D** 12   **E** 18

17 Here is a treasure map. A pirate is standing in the 'Start' square facing South and wants to
reach the treasure by following the marked route.

**Which directions should
the pirate follow to
reach the treasure?**

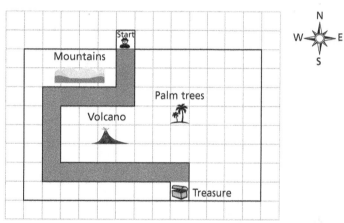

A FORWARD 3, TURN RIGHT 90°, FORWARD 5, TURN LEFT 90°, FORWARD 4, TURN LEFT 90°,
FORWARD 7, TURN RIGHT 90°, FORWARD 2

B FORWARD 3, TURN RIGHT 90°, FORWARD 4, TURN RIGHT 90°, FORWARD 4, TURN LEFT 90°,
FORWARD 7, TURN LEFT 90°, FORWARD 1

C FORWARD 3, TURN LEFT 90°, FORWARD 4, TURN LEFT 90°, FORWARD 4, TURN RIGHT 90°,
FORWARD 7, TURN RIGHT 90°, FORWARD 3

D FORWARD 3, TURN RIGHT 90°, FORWARD 4, TURN LEFT 90°, FORWARD 4, TURN LEFT 90°,
FORWARD 7, TURN RIGHT 90°, FORWARD 1

E FORWARD 3, TURN RIGHT 90°, FORWARD 4, TURN RIGHT 90°, FORWARD 5, TURN LEFT 90°,
FORWARD 8, TURN RIGHT 90°, FORWARD 1

18 Shenara takes a train to London. The train comes into London at 16.15. The journey took 75 minutes.

At what time did her journey start?

A 3.00 pm   **B** 3.45 pm   **C** 5.00 pm   **D** 5.15 pm   **E** 2.00 pm

19 Here is a Venn diagram showing multiples of 4 and factors of 72.

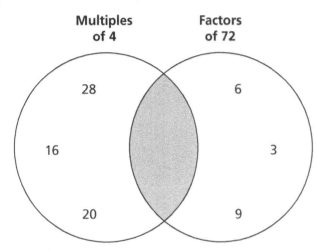

Multiples of 4   **Factors of 72**

28   6

16   3

20   9

Which number could go in the shaded region of the diagram?

A 7   **B** 2   **C** 8   **D** 14   **E** 40

20 An aeroplane flies at 740 kilometres per hour.

How far does it fly in 8.5 hours?

A 5890 km   **B** 6550 km   **C** 5920 km   **D** 6290 km   **E** 5620 km

21 What is $\frac{1}{3} + \frac{4}{9}$?

A $\frac{13}{27}$ **B** $\frac{5}{12}$ **C** $\frac{5}{9}$ **D** $\frac{3}{12}$ **E** $\frac{7}{9}$

22 This graph shows the number of times a new song was streamed over six months.

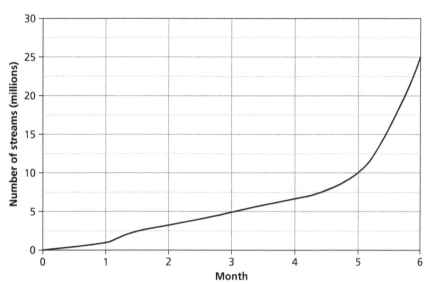

In which month was the song streamed approximately twice as much as it was streamed in Month 3?

A Month 1 **B** Month 2 **C** Month 4 **D** Month 5 **E** Month 6

23 Broccoli costs £0.30 per 100 g.

How much does 250 g cost?

A £0.75 **B** £0.60 **C** £2.50 **D** £0.25 **E** £1.30

24 Ella makes this shape out of blocks. This is the front view of the shape:

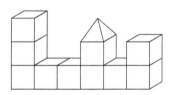

Which of the following shows the rear view of the shape?

A
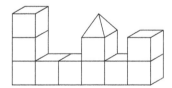

B
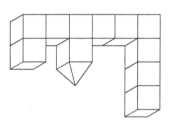

C
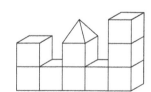

D
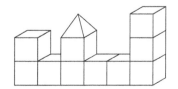

E

25 Which number is 70% of 40?

A 35   B 28   C 7   D 14   E 10

26 Which of these measurements is mostly likely to be the height of a door in a house?

A 21 cm   B 2.1 cm   C 21 m   D 2.1 m   E 210 mm

27 Which of these values is the largest?

A 68%   B 0.68   C 0.608   D 6.8%   E $\frac{6}{8}$

28 The diameter of a circle is 24 cm.

How far is the distance from the centre of the circle to the circumference?

A 48 cm   B 24 cm   C 12 cm   D 10 cm   E 6 cm

29 James is replacing the skirting board in his bedroom.
He needs to have it along the full length of each wall.
A plan of the bedroom is shown.

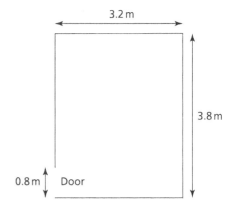

What length of skirting board does he need?

A 10.8 m   B 13.2 m   C 7.0 m   D 10.2 m   E 7.8 m

30

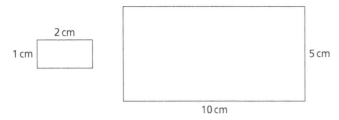

How many of the smaller rectangles can fit into the larger rectangle?

A 20   B 25   C 30   D 50   E 10

31

The 'A' shape is reflected in the *y*-axis.

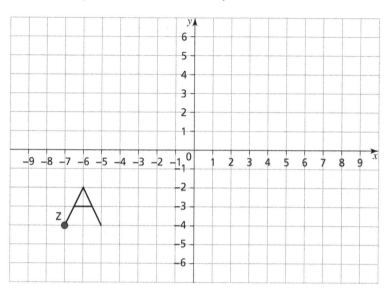

What are the co-ordinates of the point Z in the reflection?

A (4, −7)   **B** (−7, −4)   **C** (7, 4)   **D** (−4, −7)   **E** (7, −4)

32

Matilda is buying new clothes. She buys a top that costs £7.20, trousers that cost £18.50, three pairs of socks that cost £2.20 each and a pair of shoes that costs £20.00.

How much has she spent?

A £44.90   **B** £52.30   **C** £47.90   **D** £45.30   **E** £32.90

33

Each row and each column in this square adds to 50.

20		17
19		☆
	21	

What number should go in the space with a star?

A 9   **B** 15   **C** 13   **D** 16   **E** 12

34

Here is a sequence made of sticks. The first three shapes of the sequence are shown.

How many sticks are needed to make the fifth shape?

A 30 sticks   **B** 21 sticks   **C** 25 sticks   **D** 29 sticks   **E** 35 sticks

35 Order the fractions from smallest to largest.

$\frac{3}{4}$ $\frac{3}{8}$ $\frac{5}{8}$ $\frac{1}{2}$ $\frac{4}{16}$

A $\frac{3}{4}$ $\frac{4}{16}$ $\frac{5}{8}$ $\frac{1}{2}$ $\frac{3}{8}$

B $\frac{1}{2}$ $\frac{3}{4}$ $\frac{3}{8}$ $\frac{5}{8}$ $\frac{4}{16}$

C $\frac{5}{8}$ $\frac{3}{4}$ $\frac{1}{2}$ $\frac{3}{8}$ $\frac{4}{16}$

D $\frac{4}{16}$ $\frac{3}{8}$ $\frac{3}{4}$ $\frac{5}{8}$ $\frac{1}{2}$

E $\frac{4}{16}$ $\frac{3}{8}$ $\frac{1}{2}$ $\frac{5}{8}$ $\frac{3}{4}$

36 Susan is filling her sand pit.

Sand is sold in boxes of $0.3\,m^3$.

How many boxes of sand does she need to completely fill the sand pit?

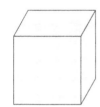

0.5 m

3 m

2 m

A   12 boxes   **B**   10 boxes   **C**   6 boxes   **D**   8 boxes   **E**   4 boxes

37 The length of each side of this cube was made 10 times longer.

How much did the volume increase by?

A   300 times   **B**   30 times   **C**   100 times   **D**   1000 times   **E**   10 times

38 Tayla asked 720 children about their favourite school dinner. She displayed the results in this pie chart.

How many more children said their favourite was fish and chips than said roast dinner?

A   150 children

B   210 children

C   300 children

D   120 children

E   100 children

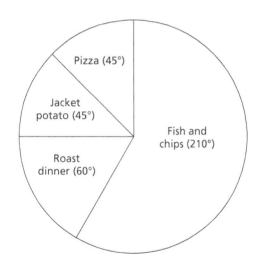

Pizza (45°)

Jacket potato (45°)

Fish and chips (210°)

Roast dinner (60°)

39 Here are three identical rhombuses:

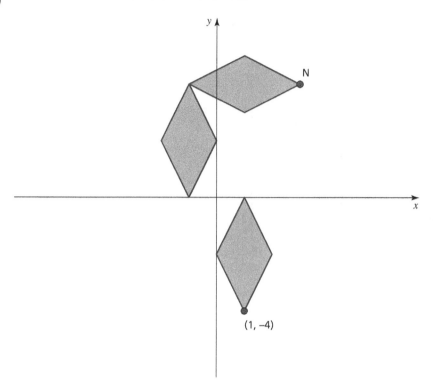

What are the co-ordinates of point N?

A (–3, –4)   B (–3, 4)   C (1, 4)   D (4, 1)   E (3, 4)

40 The area of a rectangle is 36 cm².

Which of these could be the perimeter of the rectangle?

A 18 cm   B 28 cm   C 36 cm   D 30 cm   E 15 cm

41 The number of faces (F), edges (E) and vertices (V) of a 3D shape are related by Euler's formula: V – E + F = 2.

This 3D shape has 12 pentagonal faces, 30 square faces and 20 triangular faces. It has 60 vertices.

How many edges does this 3D shape have?

A 62 edges

B 60 edges

C 120 edges

D 122 edges

E 110 edges

42 Here is a chart showing the amount of time Louis spends playing outside each day.

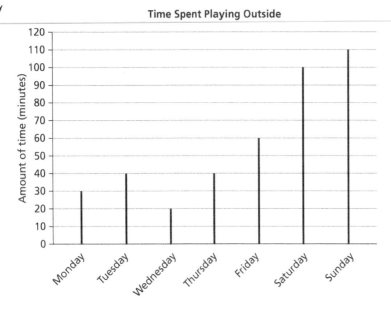

Time Spent Playing Outside

Using the mean, how much more time, on average, does he spend outside on the weekend than on the weekdays?

A 87 minutes   B 40 minutes   C 52 minutes   D 73 minutes   E 67 minutes

43 Here is a sorting diagram showing some properties of quadrilaterals.

	All sides equal	Not all sides equal
At least two sides are parallel	1	2
No parallel sides	3	4

In which section of the diagram does a trapezium belong?

A Section 1   B Section 2

C Section 3   D Section 4

E It does not belong on the diagram.

44 Daisy has started making a flower bed in the way shown below. The flower bed will be 2.8 metres long and separated into sections for different types of flowers. Each section will be made up of a 50 cm long board with a 5 cm divider between each section and on each end.

How many boards and how many dividers does she need?

A 4 boards and 6 dividers

B 5 boards and 6 dividers

C 5 boards and 5 dividers

D 4 boards and 5 dividers

E 6 boards and 4 dividers

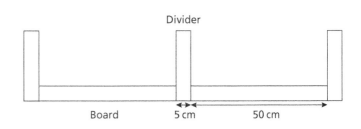

Divider

Board   5 cm   50 cm

45 Here is a rhombus.

What is the size of the shaded angle?

A 35°   B 150°   C 90°

D 135°   E 120°

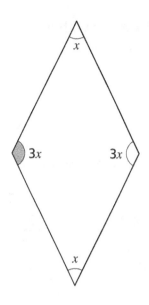

46 Here is a table showing the favourite sports of children in two classes.

	Football	Rugby	Dodgeball	Total
Giraffe Class	12	10		30
Zebra Class	7			
Total	19	18	20	

How many children in Zebra Class said their favourite was dodgeball?

A 12 children   B 24 children   C 18 children   D 16 children   E 15 children

47 So-Much-Sugar makes sugar cubes that measure 1 cm on all sides. Each cube weighs 2.3 g. The cubes ship in cartons that are 15 cm wide, 5 cm deep and 10 cm long.

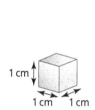
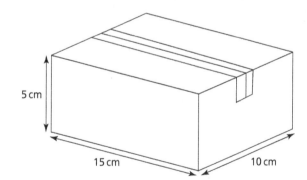

What weight of sugar is in a full carton?

A 1725 kg   B 17.25 kg   C 172.5 g   D 1.725 kg   E 17.25 g

48 Here is part of a shape with a given line of symmetry:

Which option shows the completed shape using the given line of symmetry?

Shape 1

Shape 2

Shape 3

Shape 4

Shape 5

A Shape 1 **B** Shape 2 **C** Shape 3 **D** Shape 4 **E** Shape 5

49 Eryn asked some people about their favourite colours and displayed the results in a pie chart. 60 people said their favourite was pink or purple.

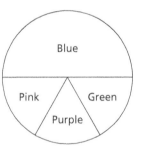

How many people did she survey?

A 300 people **B** 360 people **C** 180 people **D** 120 people **E** 240 people

50 Aayan records his 200 m run times. After five runs, his mean time is 41 seconds. After six runs, his mean time is 40 seconds.

What was his time on the sixth run?

A 35 seconds **B** 40 seconds **C** 45 seconds **D** 41 seconds **E** 24 seconds

END OF PAPER

Collins

Mathematics Multiple Choice Practice Paper 3

Read these instructions carefully:

1. You must not open or turn over this booklet until you are told to do so.

2. This booklet is a multiple-choice test containing different types of questions.

3. Do all rough working on a separate sheet of paper.

4. You should mark your answers in pencil on the answer sheet provided, not on this booklet.

5. Rub out any mistakes as well as you can and mark your new answer.

6. Try to do as many questions as you can. If you find that you cannot do a question, do not waste time on it but go on to the next one.

7. If you are stuck on a question, choose the answer that you think is best.

8. You have 50 minutes to complete the test.

1 Choose the option that shows this number in figures:

twenty thousand five hundred and thirteen

A 200 513   **B** 20 530   **C** 25 013   **D** 2513   **E** 20 513

2 A crisps company asks people about their favourite flavour of crisps. This pictogram shows the results.

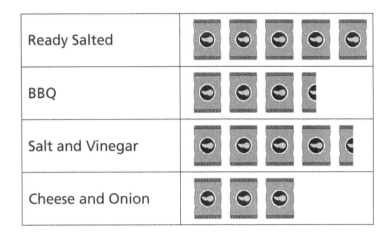 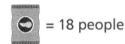

How many more people said they like salt and vinegar than said they like cheese and onion?

A 6 people   **B** 12 people   **C** 27 people   **D** 9 people   **E** 18 people

3 What is 7.327 metres rounded to the nearest centimetre?

A 732 cm   **B** 733 cm   **C** 73 cm   **D** 73.3 cm   **E** 73.2 cm

4 Which type of angle is shown?

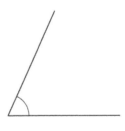

A Obtuse   **B** Acute   **C** Reflex

D Right angle   **E** Straight angle

5 Jadyn is baking cakes for his class cake sale. He buys 5 bags of flour. Each bag of flour weighs 500 g.

How many kilograms of flour did he buy?

A 25 kg   **B** 2500 kg   **C** 250 kg   **D** 2.5 kg   **E** 0.25 kg

6 Here are five shapes:

Shape 1 Shape 2 Shape 3 Shape 4 Shape 5

Which shape is not a hexagon?

A Shape 1   **B** Shape 2   **C** Shape 3   **D** Shape 4   **E** Shape 5

7 **Given that 552 × 35 = 19320, what is 1104 × 35?**

A 38640   **B** 9660   **C** 35870   **D** 35000   **E** 9770

8 Five children compete in a 1km run. Their times are shown in this table.

Child	Time (minutes)
Ana	10
Bilal	12
Charlie	9
Diane	8
Emilia	11

What is the mean race time?

A 9 minutes   **B** 11 minutes   **C** 12 minutes   **D** 10 minutes   **E** 8 minutes

9 Mrs Smart is making squash to serve at a party. She needs to fill 30 cups and plans to put 125ml in each cup.

How many litres of squash does she need to make?

A 0.35 litres   **B** 5 litres   **C** 150 litres   **D** 1.25 litres   **E** 3.75 litres

10 Here is a sequence of numbers:

524   518   ☐   506   500

What is the missing term?

A 516   **B** 520   **C** 512   **D** 504   **E** 530

11 Here is a graph showing the height of a Great Dane from 2 months to 7 months old.

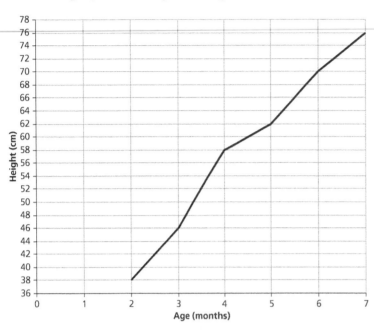

In which period did the Great Dane grow the least?

A 2 months to 3 months

B 3 months to 4 months

C 4 months to 5 months

D 5 months to 6 months

E 6 months to 7 months

12 What is the volume of the cuboid?

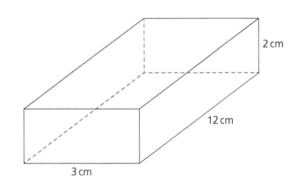

A 24 cm³   **B** 68 cm³   **C** 17 cm³

D 36 cm³   **E** 72 cm³

13 This bar chart shows the results of a survey about children's favourite seasons.

How many children were surveyed?

A 28   **B** 34   **C** 16

D 50   **E** 30

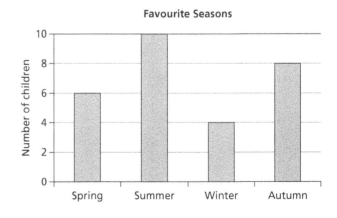

14
What is the missing number in this calculation?

$397 \div \boxed{} = 3.97$

A 0.01   **B** 10   **C** 1000   **D** 0.1   **E** 100

15
The pie chart shows the proportion of children who said they prefer different types of sweets.

Which type of sweets did the most number of children prefer?

A Gummy Bears   **B** Lollies   **C** Chocolates

D Toffees   **E** Other

16
What are the co-ordinates of the point Z shown on the grid?

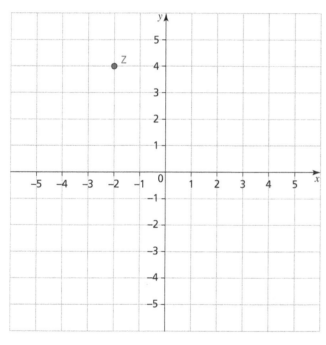

A (2, –4)   **B** (2, 4)   **C** (–2, 4)   **D** (4, –2)   **E** (4, 2)

17
Miss B's class grew sunflowers from seeds. They measured the height of the plants at the end of each week.

Week	Week 1	Week 2	Week 3	Week 4	Week 5	Week 6
Height	2 cm	10 cm	15 cm	25 cm	30 cm	38 cm

During which period did the sunflower grow the most?

A Week 1 to Week 2   **B** Week 2 to Week 3   **C** Week 3 to Week 4

D Week 4 to Week 5   **E** Week 5 to Week 6

18 A children's performance lasts for 75 minutes. The performance finishes at 3.30pm.

When did the performance start?

A 14.15   B 15.15   C 04.50   D 03.00   E 14.30

19 This chart shows some children's favourite fruit.

How many more children said their favourite fruit was either bananas or apples than said grapes?

A 15 children

B 30 children

C 20 children

D 25 children

E 5 children

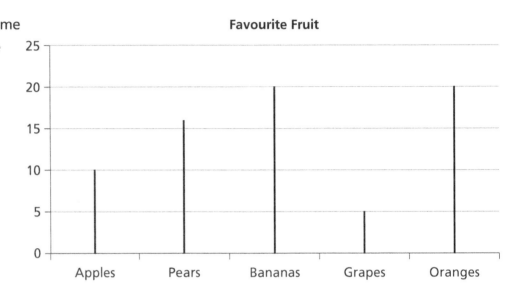

Favourite Fruit

20 **Order these values from smallest to biggest:**

| 34% | $\frac{1}{20}$ | $\frac{3}{50}$ | 0.36 | 8.4% |

A 0.36   34% $\frac{3}{50}$ $\frac{1}{20}$ 8.4%

B 8.4% $\frac{3}{50}$ $\frac{1}{20}$ 34%   0.36

C 0.36 $\frac{3}{50}$ $\frac{1}{20}$ 8.4%   34%

D $\frac{1}{20}$ 8.4%   0.36 $\frac{3}{50}$ 34%

E $\frac{1}{20}$ $\frac{3}{50}$ 8.4%   34%   0.36

21 What is $\frac{13}{16} - \frac{1}{8}$?

A $\frac{11}{16}$ B $\frac{12}{8}$ C $1\frac{1}{4}$ D $\frac{12}{16}$ E $1\frac{3}{16}$

22 Here is a map of the grounds of a school. The position of Sonny is shown.

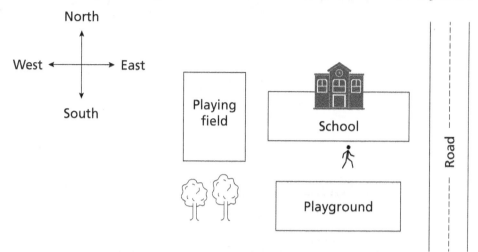

Sonny is facing due East. He makes a three-quarter turn clockwise.

What is in front of him?

A Road   B School   C Playground   D Playing field   E Trees

23 The timetable for a train between Birmingham and Leamington Spa is shown.

Birmingham	19.17	19.50	20.08
Solihull	19.25	19.59	---------
Dorridge	---------	---------	---------
Warwick	19.35	---------	20.26
Leamington Spa	19.41	20.14	20.31

Oliver takes the train that leaves Birmingham at 20.08.

How long does it take him to get to Warwick?

A 48 minutes   B 18 minutes   C 26 minutes   D 31 minutes   E 50 minutes

24 42 people are on a bus. There are twice as many men as women.

How many men are on the bus?

A 35   B 14   C 7   D 21   E 28

25 What is the size of angle x?

A 140°
B 130°
C 115°
D 180°
E 80°

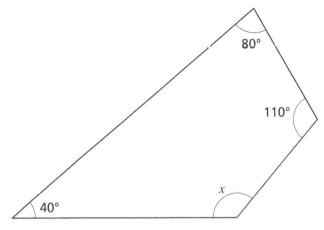

26 Here is a partially complete two-way table:

	Blue eyes	Green eyes	Brown eyes
Girls	5	7	
Boys	2		8
Total		12	16

How many boys were surveyed?

A 15   B 7   C 12   D 10   E 28

27 Complete the calculation.

$(43 \times 817) + (57 \times 817) =$ ☐

A 81 700   B 35 131   C 73 530   D 163 400   E 8710

28 Here is a bar chart showing the ways in which children go to school. The y-axis does not have a scale shown. 100 children were surveyed.

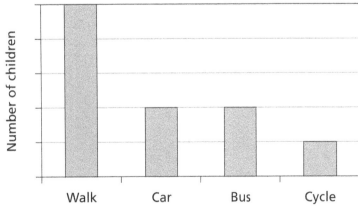

How many children walk to school?

A 20   B 80   C 5   D 10   E 50

29 Entrance to a theme park costs £23 for children. It costs twice as much for adults.

How much would it cost for a group of 4 children and 2 adults to go to the theme park?

A £138.00   B £184.00   C £276.00   D £143.00   E £92.00

30 **Which of the following nets will fold up to make a triangular-based pyramid?**

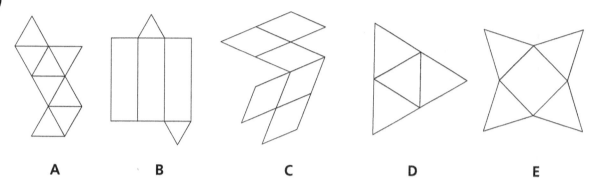

A   B   C   D   E

31 **How many 20p coins are needed to make £16.00?**

A 80 coins   B 40 coins   C 20 coins   D 160 coins   E 10 coins

32 Mahmud asked 184 children about their favourite sport. One in four said their favourite was football.

Which calculation can be used to find the number of children who said their favourite was football?

A 184 ÷ 25% =

B 184 × 0.75 =

C 184 × 0.25 =

D 184 ÷ $\frac{1}{5}$ =

E 184 ÷ $\frac{1}{4}$ =

33 The graph shows a population of rabbits over time.

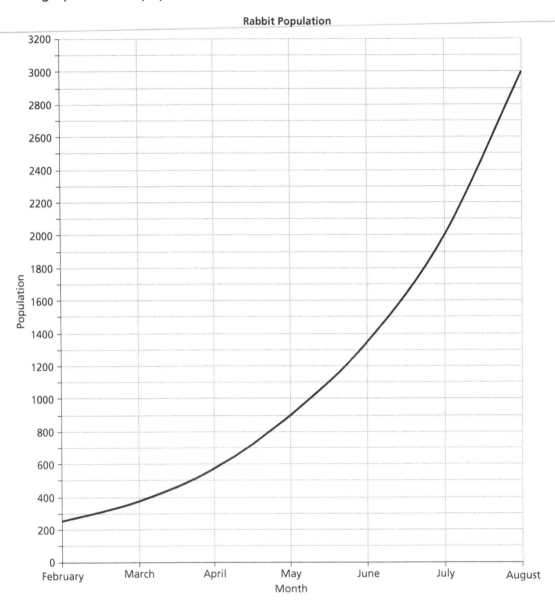

Rabbit Population

Approximately how many fewer rabbits were there in May than in July?

A 1000   B 1100   C 2000   D 1500   E 500

34 Malcolm is buying groceries. He buys bananas that cost £2.20 per bunch, carrots that cost £1.20, pasta that costs £2.00 and sauce that costs £1.30. He pays with a £10 note.

How much change does he get?

A £6.70   B £3.30   C £1.70   D £2.80   E £5.50

35 Annabel kept track of the birds she saw in her garden in one day. She saw 24 birds.

This pie chart shows the results.

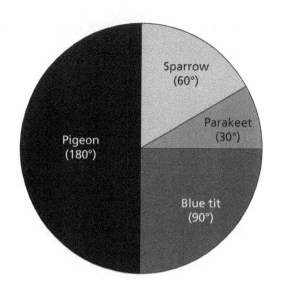

How many more sparrows than parakeets did she see?

A 2   B 4   C 8   D 10   E 15

36 Brigitte looks at this thermometer in her garden at 8.30 pm and sees the reading shown. At 3.00 am it is 15°C cooler.

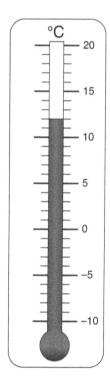

What temperature is it at 3.00 am?

A −5°C   B 3°C   C −3°C   D 5°C   E 7°C

37 Najih drives 180 miles from Oxford to Liverpool. It takes him 3 hours.

What is his average speed in miles per hour?

A 40 mph   B 70 mph   C 80 mph   D 60 mph   E 50 mph

38 The L-shape on the grid is reflected in the *x*-axis.

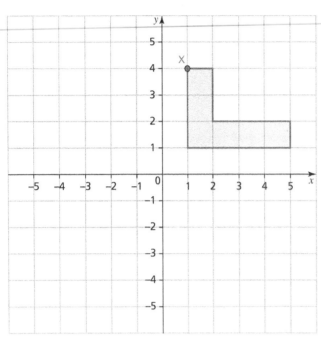

What are the co-ordinates of the point X in the reflection?

A (1, −4)   B (−1, −4)   C (−4, −1)   D (1, 4)   E (4, 1)

39 The table shows the number of pupils with blue eyes in a junior school.

Year group	Year 3	Year 4	Year 5	Year 6
Number of pupils	5	6		3

Abdul finds the mean of the number of pupils with blue eyes to be 5.

How many pupils in Year 5 have blue eyes?

A 5 pupils   B 7 pupils   C 10 pupils   D 6 pupils   E 4 pupils

40 James is twice as old as Henry. Henry is three years older than Ingrid. Ingrid is 18.

How old is James?

A 18   B 30   C 15   D 20   E 42

41 Mrs Scott is replacing the flooring in her kitchen.
A plan of the kitchen is shown.

What area of flooring does she need to buy?

A 1 m²
B 6 m²
C 4 m²
D 5 m²
E 7 m²

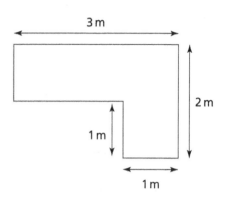

42 Tricia wrote down a sequence counting up in 8s. She started at a number between 50 and 60 and finished at the number 77.

What was the first number in her sequence?

A 57   B 51   C 53   D 56   E 55

43 Here is a triangle:

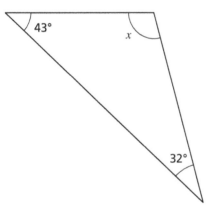

What is the size of angle *x*?

A 285°   B 110°   C 75°   D 105°   E 215°

44 Tiana takes the bus to a friend's house. Her journey takes one quarter of an hour. She arrives at her friend's house at 15.40.

At what time did she leave home?

A 2.00 am   B 3.15 pm   C 3.25 pm   D 2.30 pm   E 3.30 pm

45 Here are five shapes:

 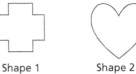 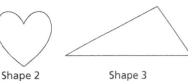 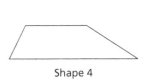 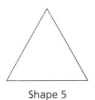

Shape 1   Shape 2   Shape 3   Shape 4   Shape 5

Which shapes do not have a line of symmetry?

A   Shape 1 and Shape 3

B   Shape 2 and Shape 4

C   Shape 4 and Shape 5

D   Shape 3 and Shape 4

E   Shape 2 and Shape 3

46 Here is a shape on a co-ordinate grid:

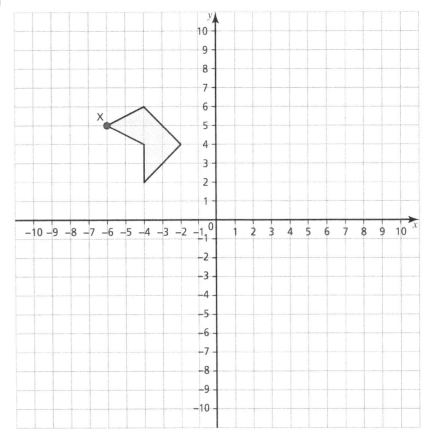

The shape is translated by 4 units to the right and 2 units down.

What are the co-ordinates of point X after the translation?

A   (4, −2)   B   (2, −4)   C   (2, −3)   D   (−3, 2)   E   (−2, 3)

47 A bottle holds 3.5 pints of milk.

How many bottles are needed to hold 42 pints of milk?

A 12   **B** 15   **C** 16   **D** 18   **E** 20

48 Here is a graph to convert between miles and kilometres:

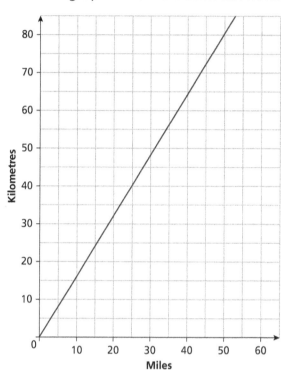

Approximately how many kilometres is 25 miles?

A 15 km   **B** 30 km   **C** 40 km   **D** 35 km   **E** 50 km

49 The table shows the heights of some children rounded to the nearest centimetre.

Height (nearest cm)	Tally	Total
120–124		4
125–129	ЖИ ЖИ III	
130–134		17
135–139	ЖИ IIII	
140–144		5
145–149		2

What percentage of children were less than 130 cm tall?

A 17%   **B** 50%   **C** 23%   **D** 34%   **E** 62%

50 Here is a triangle on a straight line:

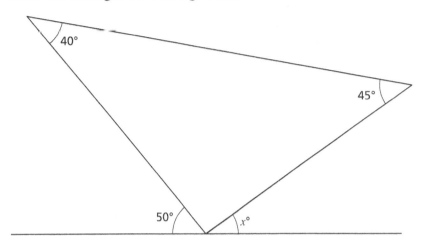

Find the size of angle x.

A   50°   B   35°   C   85°   D   100°   E   130°

END OF PAPER

Collins

Mathematics Multiple Choice Practice Paper 4

Read these instructions carefully:

1. You must not open or turn over this booklet until you are told to do so.

2. This booklet is a multiple-choice test containing different types of questions.

3. Do all rough working on a separate sheet of paper.

4. You should mark your answers in pencil on the answer sheet provided, not on this booklet.

5. Rub out any mistakes as well as you can and mark your new answer.

6. Try to do as many questions as you can. If you find that you cannot do a question, do not waste time on it but go on to the next one.

7. If you are stuck on a question, choose the answer that you think is best.

8. You have 50 minutes to complete the test.

1 What is the value of 2 in this number?

82 537

A 2 tens   B 2 hundreds   C 2 thousands   D 2 ones   E 2 ten thousands

2 Here is a pictogram showing some children's favourite superheroes:

Amazing A	★★◗
Mr Blast	★★★
Super C	★★★◗
Dr Dark	★★★★
Electric E	★★★★◗

★ = 6 children

How many more children said their favourite was Dr Dark than said Amazing A?

A 18 children   B 9 children   C 15 children   D 24 children   E 12 children

3 Here is a kite:

What is the sum of the interior angles of the kite?

A 90°   B 120°   C 180°   D 270°   E 360°

4 What amount of money is 5% of £5?

A 5p   B 25p   C 1p   D 50p   E 10p

5 What is the missing number in this calculation?

$493 \div \boxed{} = 0.493$

A 10   B 100   C 1000   D 0.1   E 0.01

6 What is the size of angle x?

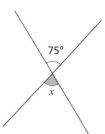

A 105° **B** 75° **C** 180° **D** 360° **E** 45°

7 Here are some numbers:

12   14   18   75   114

Which statement about these numbers is true?

A They are all prime numbers.
B They are all composite numbers.
C They are all multiples of 3.
D They are all even numbers.
E They are all two-digit numbers.

8 A map of a neighbourhood is shown.

Aaliyah is standing with the fountain on her right and can see the school straight ahead.

In which direction is she facing?

A North **B** South-West **C** West

D South-East **E** East

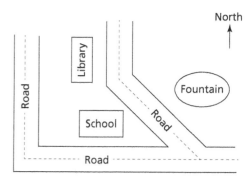

9 **Which of these calculations gives a different answer from the others?**

A $\frac{3}{4}$ of 50 **B** 50% of 75 **C** 0.75 × 50 **D** 0.50 × 75 **E** $\frac{1}{4}$ × 50

10 Here is part of a shape with a given line of symmetry:

Which shape is made by completing the shape with the given line of symmetry?

A Rectangle **B** Trapezium **C** Rhombus

D Hexagon **E** Triangle

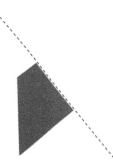

11 Mr Apell has 1.2 litres of paint that he is separating into equal pots of 80 ml for each student.

How many pots can he fill?

A 15   B 30   C 40

D 13   E 8

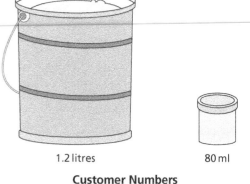

1.2 litres   80 ml

12 A telephone company displayed the number of customers it has had over time, in thousands, on this misleading graph.

What makes the graph misleading?

A The scale on the y-axis is uneven.
B The scale on the x-axis is uneven.
C The points are connected.
D Year is not a good label for the x-axis.
E The number of customers is not a good label for the y-axis.

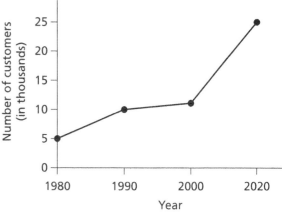

13 Here is a time graph showing Larissa's journey:

Which of the following descriptions could the graph show?

A She travels directly to a friend's house at a constant speed before turning back immediately towards home.

B She travels directly to a friend's house at a constant speed, stays for a while and heads home.

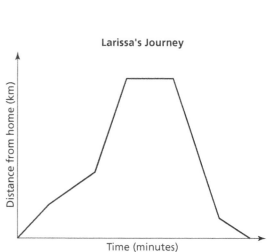

C She travels directly to a friend's house at a constant speed, stays for a while and continues on her journey away from home.

D She travels at a varying speed to a friend's house before immediately turning around and going home.

E She travels at a varying speed to a friend's house, stays for a while and heads home at a varying speed.

14 Stephen is buying some groceries. He buys three apples, two bunches of bananas and one bag of carrots. The grocery prices are shown opposite. He has £5.

Which of the following calculations show how he could reasonably estimate if he has enough money?

A (0.3 × 3) + (1.2 × 2) + 2
B (30 × 2) + (1.2 × 2) + 2
C (0.2 × 3) + (1 × 2) + 2
D (20 × 2) + (100 × 2) + 2
E (30 × 2) + (120 × 2) + 2

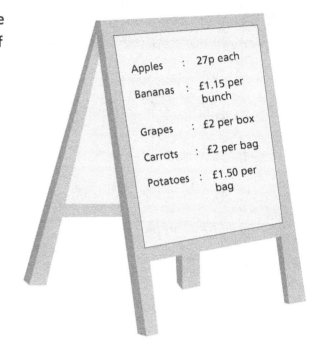

Apples   : 27p each
Bananas : £1.15 per bunch
Grapes   : £2 per box
Carrots   : £2 per bag
Potatoes : £1.50 per bag

15 The bar chart shows some children's favourite toys.

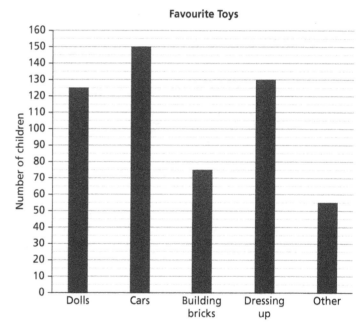

Favourite Toys

How many more children said 'cars' or 'dolls' than said 'building bricks'?

A 100   B 75   C 175   D 200   E 50

16 Mrs Honey's class has 28 children. There are three times as many girls as boys.

How many girls are in the class?

A 7   B 21   C 14   D 12   E 25

17 Jennifer takes a bus to get home from work. She gets on the bus at 17.51. When she arrives at her bus stop, she looks at her watch and sees the time shown here.

How long was her journey?

A   57 minutes

B   74 minutes

C   43 minutes

D   1 hour 30 minutes

E   32 minutes

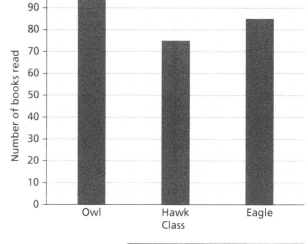

Reading Challenge

18 A primary school is completing a reading challenge for each year group to read 300 books. The results of the three Year 5 classes after one month are shown in this bar chart.

How many more books does Year 5 need to read to reach 300 books?

A 100 books   B 55 books   C 45 books

D 75 books   E 60 books

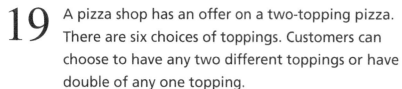

19 A pizza shop has an offer on a two-topping pizza. There are six choices of toppings. Customers can choose to have any two different toppings or have double of any one topping.

PIZZA TOPPINGS

- Pepperoni
- Sausage
- Mushrooms
- Onions
- Peppers
- Olives

How many different pizza combinations can be created?

A   12   B   6   C   21   D   15   E   18

20 The students in a junior school compete in a trivia challenge. Their scores for each round are shown in the table.

	Round 1	Round 2	Round 3	Round 4
Year 3	12	15	8	14
Year 4	17	13	14	10
Year 5	12	14	11	11
Year 6	9	12	17	10

What is the mean score for Year 5?

A 10   **B** 8   **C** 12   **D** 14   **E** 16

21 One day on Jupiter is 9 hours and 56 minutes.

How many seconds are in one day on Jupiter?

A 35 760   **B** 86 400   **C** 32 400   **D** 36 000   **E** 91 300

22 Some children were asked their favourite type of music. This pictogram shows the results.

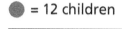

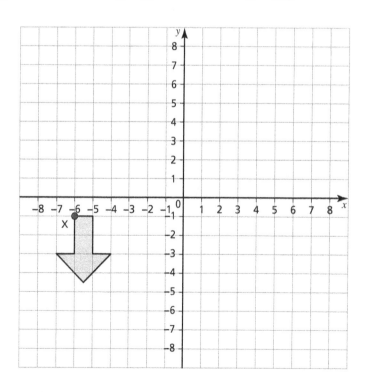

How many fewer children said 'classical' than said 'hip-hop' or 'pop'?

A 30   **B** 12   **C** 90   **D** 42   **E** 126

23 The shape shown on the grid is translated by 3 up and 7 to the right.

What are the co-ordinates of point X after the translation?

A (−13, −4)

B (−8, −4)

C (1, −4)

D (1, 2)

E (−8, 2)

24 Elsie is baking cupcakes. Part of the recipe is shown.

She needs to make 36 cupcakes.

How much sugar should she use?

A 250g   B 275g   C 375g

D 320g   E 500g

Recipe	
Makes 24 cupcakes	
250g	butter
250g	sugar
50ml	milk
2	eggs
…	…

25 Mr Tanner is repaving his drive using bricks. His drive measures 3.6 metres wide by 4.8 metres long. Each brick is 100mm long by 200mm wide. He plans to cover the drive by laying the bricks in rows across the drive similar to the pattern shown.

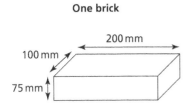

One brick

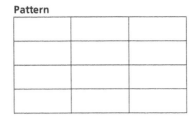

Pattern

Which of the following calculations shows how many bricks he needs to buy?

A 36 × 48 =   B 3600 × 4800 =   C 18 × 24 =   D 18 × 48 =   E 3.6 × 4.8 =

26 Poppy has £1.87 in coins.

Which of the following does not show a combination of coins she could have?

A

B

C

D

E

27 What is the value of x in the equation $x \div 15 = 5$?

A 75   B 90   C 60   D 15   E 10

28 The pie charts give information about the timeliness of two different train operators.

Company A

Company B

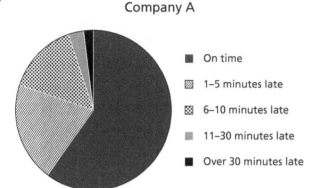
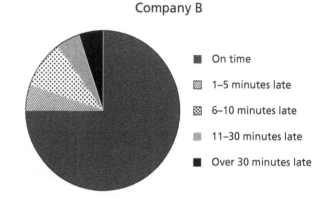

Which of these statements must be true based on the pie charts?

A Company B has more trains that are over 30 minutes late than Company A.
B Company B runs fewer trains than Company A.
C Company B runs more trains than Company A.
D Company A cancels a lot of trains.
E Company B has a higher proportion of trains that are on-time than Company A.

29 William wrote down a sequence counting down in 6s. He started at a number between 60 and 65 and finished at the number 45.

What was the first number in his sequence?

A 64   B 60   C 61   D 63   E 62

30 Martine is designing a heptagonal-based pyramid out of card. She wants each face to be a different colour.

How many different colours of card does she need?

A 7   B 8   C 10   D 6   E 9

31 Miriam is designing a cloth lampshade in the shape of a regular octagonal prism which will be open on both ends. The lampshade will be 20 cm long and each side will be 80 mm wide.

What area of cloth will she need?

A 1600 cm²   B 128 m²   C 160 cm²   D 12.8 m²   E 1280 cm²

32 Wilma is sending a large parcel. The courier will only take parcels with a volume of less than 0.25 m³ so she measures her parcel and finds it is 60 cm wide, 20 cm high and 50 cm deep.

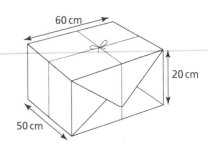

What is the volume of her parcel in cubic metres?

    A 15 m³   **B** 130 m³   **C** 60 m³   **D** 0.06 m³   **E** 0.15 m³

33 Each row and column in this square adds to 27.

What number should go in the space with a star?

    A 7   **B** 19   **C** 9   **D** 14   **E** 12

34 **What is 65.06 + 8.062?**

    A 73.068   **B** 73.662   **C** 73.062   **D** 73.122   **E** 73.014

35 Hot dogs come in packs of 6 and buns come in packs of 8.

What is the smallest number of packs of hot dogs and of buns you can buy to have the same number of buns and hot dogs?

    A 14 packs of hot dogs and 14 packs of buns
    B 3 packs of hot dogs and 4 packs of buns
    C 4 packs of hot dogs and 3 packs of buns
    D 6 packs of hot dogs and 6 packs of buns
    E 6 packs of hot dogs and 8 packs of buns

36 Lily is saving up to buy a trampoline that costs £110. She saves £15 per month. So far she has saved £45.

How many more months does she need to save in order to have enough money to buy the trampoline?

    A 10 months   **B** 4 months   **C** 3 months   **D** 5 months   **E** 8 months

37 Trenton makes a design using equilateral triangles and a trapezium.

What is the size of angle x?

    A 60°   **B** 120°   **C** 270°   **D** 240°   **E** 315°

38 A Year 6 class sold 200 cakes in a cake sale. Each cake cost them 15p to make. They sold the cakes for 50p each.

How much profit did they make in the cake sale (after they paid the cost to make the cakes)?

A £100   **B** £35   **C** £150   **D** £70   **E** £200

39 A show starts at quarter to 4 in the afternoon. It finishes at 16.27.

How long is the show?

A 12 minutes   **B** 15 minutes   **C** 75 minutes   **D** 31 minutes   **E** 42 minutes

40 Abdul is programming a robot to travel on a path in the park. The robot is facing due East to begin. A plan of the park is shown here and the path is marked.

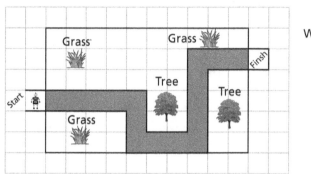

Which instructions must he give the robot to find its way through the course?

A FORWARD 5, TURN RIGHT 90°, FORWARD 2, TURN RIGHT 90°, FORWARD 3, TURN LEFT 90°, FORWARD 4, TURN RIGHT 90°, FORWARD 4

B FORWARD 5, TURN RIGHT 90°, FORWARD 2, TURN LEFT 90°, FORWARD 3, TURN RIGHT 90°, FORWARD 4, TURN LEFT 90°, FORWARD 3

C FORWARD 5, TURN RIGHT 90°, FORWARD 2, TURN LEFT 90°, FORWARD 3, TURN LEFT 90°, FORWARD 4, TURN RIGHT 90°, FORWARD 3

D FORWARD 5, TURN LEFT 90°, FORWARD 2, TURN LEFT 90°, FORWARD 3, TURN LEFT 90°, FORWARD 4, TURN RIGHT 90°, FORWARD 5

E FORWARD 5, TURN RIGHT 90°, FORWARD 2, TURN LEFT 90°, FORWARD 4, TURN LEFT 90°, FORWARD 4, TURN LEFT 90°, FORWARD 3

41 Larmor is collecting stamps. There are 48 to collect. He has $\frac{1}{3}$ of them.

How many does he have left to collect?

A 20   **B** 16   **C** 40   **D** 8   **E** 32

42 Maria is 4 feet and 10 inches tall. Naseem is 1.53 m tall.

Approximately how much taller is Naseem than Maria?

(1 inch is approximately 2.5 cm. There are 12 inches in 1 foot.)

A 8 cm   B 30 cm   C 95 cm

D 26 cm   E 10 cm

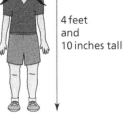

1.53 m tall

4 feet and 10 inches tall

Naseem   Maria

43 Brianna is redesigning her garden. She will lay lawn turf covering the garden, except for a path through the middle, leading from the house. Lawn turf is sold in a length of 1 m and a width of 50 cm. Each roll costs £2.97.

Approximately how much will the lawn turf cost for the garden?

A £42   B £54   C £84

D £90   E £108

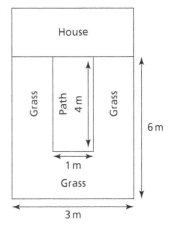

House

Grass | Path 4 m | Grass

6 m

1 m

Grass

3 m

44 A taxi firm charges a base rate of £5 plus an extra £0.15 per mile.

Which expression shows the cost to travel x miles?

A $5 + 0.15x$ B $5.15x$ C $5x + 0.15$ D $5.15 + x$ E $5.15 \times x$

45 The time graph shows Jan's drive from Leeds to Newcastle upon Tyne.

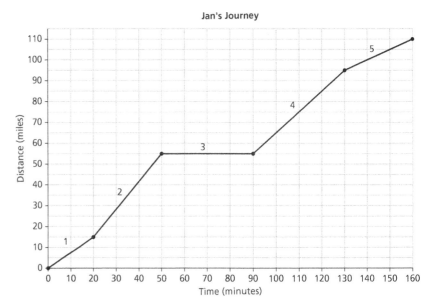

Jan's Journey

How much faster was he driving in section 4 than in section 5 on the graph?

A 40 mph   B 30 mph   C 10 mph   D 50 mph   E 70 mph

46 Pink paint is made in a ratio of one part red paint to four parts of white paint.

How much white paint is needed to make 2 litres of pink paint?

A 200 ml   B 1500 ml   C 400 ml   D 800 ml   E 1600 ml

47 Tilly and seven friends went for a meal.
Part of their bill is shown here.

	Bill		
Drinks	-------	@ £3.20	-------
Mains	8	@ £7.80	£62.40
Service charge			£9.80
Total			£88.20

How many drinks did they order?

A 7   B 12   C 10   D 8   E 5

48 Here is a parallelogram on a straight line:

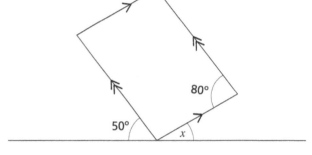

What is the size of angle *x*?

A 45°   B 30°   C 50°   D 90°   E 100°

49 A pallet box can hold 20 packages of toilet roll. There are 9 rolls in each package.

How many pallet boxes are needed to hold 3700 rolls of toilet roll?

A 21   B 24   C 18   D 20   E 25

50 The co-ordinates of the four vertices of a shape are:

(*a*, 5)   (*a* + 2, 5)   (*a* – 2, 0)   (*a* + 2, 0)

What shape is this?

A Isosceles triangle   B Trapezium   C Rectangle

D Scalene triangle   E Kite

END OF PAPER

Answers

Number and Place Value
Page 9: Quick Test
1. 10065
2. Three hundred and seventy thousand, eight hundred and six
3. a) £224950
   The 4 in the tens column rounds up to 5 because the digit to the right is 5 or more. All digits to the right of the tens column change to zero.

   b) £225000
   The 4 in the thousands column rounds up to 5 because the digit to the right is 5 or more. All digits to the right of the thousands column change to zero.

   c) £200000
   The 2 in the hundred thousands column remains unchanged since the digit to the right is less than 5. All digits to the right of the hundred thousands column change to zero.
4. E
   Newcastle has the highest negative value.
5. 342950
   342951
   349808
   359806
   359845   An alternative answer here is '9'.
   The numbers are increasing in value from top to bottom so there is only one possible answer for the missing digits in the first four numbers.

Calculations
Page 14: Quick Test
1. 34
   $180 - (45 + 40 + 61) = 34$
2. 84
   $200 - (67 + 49) = 84$
3. 44
   $308 \div 7 = 44$
4. 3024
   $252 \times 12 = 3024$
5. $(76 - 48) \div (12 \div 3) = 7$
   Working out the brackets gives
   $28 \div 4 = 7$

Page 17: Quick Test
1. E
   12 and 16 are multiples of 4, and 15 is a multiple of 5.
2. Four
   1, 4, 9, 36 are factors of 36 and are also square numbers.
3. 450 seconds
   Find the lowest common multiple of 45 and 50.

4.

10	20	6
8	12	16
18	4	14

Each row and each column adds up to 36.
5. 10
   Carry out the inverse operations:
   $(55 + 8 - 3) \div 6 = 10$

Fractions, Decimals and Percentages
Page 20: Quick Test
1. $\frac{1}{2}$ $\frac{11}{20}$ $\frac{7}{10}$ $\frac{3}{4}$ $\frac{4}{5}$
   Convert to fractions with a common denominator (of 20) in order to compare.
2. $\frac{2}{8}$ and $\frac{3}{4}$
   $\frac{3}{4}$ is equivalent to $\frac{6}{8}$ and $\frac{2}{8} + \frac{6}{8} = 1$
3. $\frac{35}{8}$
   Multiply the 4 wholes by the denominator, then add the numerator:
   $4 \times 8 + 3 = 35$
4. $\frac{6}{9}$ or $\frac{2}{3}$
   The prime numbers in the list are 3, 5, 7, 11, 13, 17. Prime numbers have two factors so 1 itself is not prime.
5. £24
   If Sunita has $\frac{3}{10}$ left after spending £56, then £56 must represent $\frac{7}{10}$ of her money. $56 \div 7 = 8$, so £8 represents $\frac{1}{10}$. £8 $\times$ 3 = £24
6. 54
   What is left in the bag is $\frac{1}{3}$ of what was there before Zoltan ate some, so that must have been 6 sweets. That is $\frac{1}{3}$ of the number in the bag before Joanna ate hers, which must have been 18. Finally, that is $\frac{1}{3}$ of what was in the bag to start with, so that must have been 54 sweets.

Page 25: Quick Test
1. A
   Convert each value to a decimal or a percentage to compare them.
2. A
   Convert each value to a decimal or a percentage to compare them.
3. C
   All the others are equivalent to 20%.
4. 75%
   21 out of 28 parts of the grid are shaded. $\frac{21}{28} = \frac{3}{4} = 75\%$

5. $\frac{3}{5}$ (or 0.6 or 60%)
   Three of the five numbers on the spinner are odd.

Ratio and Proportion
Page 28: Quick Test
1. C
   Unlike the others, 24:16 does not simplify to a ratio of 4:3.
2. 48
   The part of the ratio representing girls, i.e. 3, stands for 18 girls. So each part of the ratio represents $18 \div 3 = 6$ individuals. Since the ratio has 8 parts in total (5 + 3), the total number of children in the choir is $6 \times 8 = 48$.
3. 14.4m
   If the model plane is 20 cm long, the real one is $20 \times 72 = 1440$ cm long. 1440 cm = 14.4m.
4. 480
   1% of 500 = 5, so 4% of 500 = 20.
   $500 - 20 = 480$
5. D
   30% of £75 is £22.50, whereas all the others are £25.
6. £1.44
   10% of £1.20 is 12p, so 20% of £1.20 is 24p.
   £1.20 + £0.24 = £1.44

Algebra
Page 32: Quick Test
1. A
   If Joyti's brother was y years old two years ago, he is now $y + 2$ years old. In another five years, he will therefore be $y + 7$ years old.
2. 1.5
   Subtract 4 from both sides: $6x = 2x + 6$
   Subtract $2x$ from both sides: $4x = 6$
   Divide both sides by 4: $x = 1.5$
3. 257
   The sequence increases in steps of 4, 8, 16, 32, 64, etc. (i.e. doubling each time), so the next number will be $129 + 128 = 257$.
4. 69
   The number of matchsticks needed is 9 (+14) 23 (+20) 43 (+26) 69. Each time, you increase by the same amount as before, plus 6: (14 + 6), (20 + 6), etc. So the answer is 69.

Page 34: Quick Test
1. E
   If Maya has 4 seeds left over from a packet of 20, she has planted 16. So $4m + 4n = 16$. Of the options available, m must equal 1 and n must equal 3.

2. There are 11 different possible totals (there are 16 possible combinations of numbers but five of these add to the same number, as shown in the table below).

		Second spinner			
	+	0	2	5	7
First spinner	1	1	3	6	8
	2	2	4	7	9
	3	3	5	8	10
	4	4	6	9	11

Measurement
Page 41: Quick Test
1. B
   4 hours + 12 hours = 16 hours
2. 5.30 pm
   The total length is: 25 minutes + 1 hour 40 minutes + 5 minutes = 2 hours 10 minutes
   2 hours 10 minutes after 3.20 pm is 5.30 pm.
3. £24
   12 × 40 minutes = 480 minutes
   480 ÷ 60 = 8 hours
   8 × £3 = £24 in total
4. D
   The scale shows 1.4 kg. Emily will add 0.8 kg, so it will read 2.2 kg afterwards.
5. 4.2 litres
   The baby drinks 600 ml of milk each day, which is 7 × 600 ml = 4200 ml of milk a week, or 4.2 l.

Page 43: Quick Test
1. a) 1.2 cm³
   Volume of cuboid =
   length × width × height =
   15 × 10 × 8 = 150 × 8 = 1200 mm³.
   There are 1000 mm³ in 1 cm³, so the answer is 1.2 cm³.

   b) 7 cm²
   There are three different kinds of faces.
   The top and base are each 15 × 10 = 150 mm²; total: 300 mm².
   The left and right faces are each 10 × 8 = 80 mm²; total: 160 mm².
   The front and back are each 15 × 8 = 120 mm²; total: 240 mm².
   Surface area = 300 + 160 + 240 = 700 mm²
   There are 100 mm² in 1 cm², so the answer is 7 cm².

2. A
   A = 10 × 6 = 60 cm²
   B = 15 × 5 = 75 cm²
   C = $\frac{1}{2}$ × 8 × 12 = 48 cm²
   D = 7² = 49 cm²
   E = 10² − $\frac{1}{2}$ × 10 × 5 = 100 − 25 = 75 cm²
   So B and E have the same area.

3. 12
   This is one way to do it:

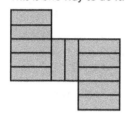

4. 40 mph
   The time taken via the first route is 14 miles ÷ 28 mph = 0.5 hours (30 mins)
   So if the 20-mile journey via the second route also takes 0.5 hours, the average speed is 20 miles ÷ 0.5 = 40 mph.

5. C
   The volume of water in the pond at the minimum depth will be:
   200 cm × 50 cm × 90 cm = 900 000 cm³
   There are 1 000 000 cm³ in 1 m³, so 900 000 cm³ = 0.9 m³ or 900 litres.
   900 ÷ 45 = 20 (this is how many fish can be accommodated in 900 litres of water)
   Zak already has 15 fish so he can buy another 5 fish.

Geometry
Page 50: Quick Test
1. Five
2. D
   Count all the edges shown in the net (19) and subtract the number of edges on a cube (12), so 19 − 12 = 7.
3. 114°
   The known angles in the kite total 42° + 90° = 132°. All the angles in the kite must add up to 360°; that leaves 360° − 132° = 228°. Kites are symmetrical, so x must be the same size as the other unknown angle on the right. So x must be 228° ÷ 2 = 114°
4. (1, 3)
5. C
   (−4, 0) and (2, 3) are exactly two units above (−4, −2) and (2, 1), which are on the line.

Statistics
Page 56: Quick Test
1. 15
   Art = 30 and Drama = 15, so 30 − 15 = 15
2. E
   Read up to the line from 1.5 kg and across to the value in pounds (3.3) on the vertical axis.
3. 165 jars
   15% of the pie chart represents 45 jars of blackcurrant jam sold, so 1% of the pie chart represents 3 jars. Strawberry jam is 55% of the pie chart (100% − 30% − 15%) and 55 × 3 = 165.
4. 6
   If the mean number of merit points scored across 12 weeks was 7, then 12 × 7 = 84 merit points were scored in total across the 12 weeks. Adding up the merit points for the first 11 weeks gives 78, so 6 must have been scored in week 12.

Pages 58–59
Practice Test 1: Number and Place Value
1. C
   The number is six thousand, five hundred and twenty-three, so there are two tens.
2. B
3. C
   The digits should be placed in ascending order, from left to right, to make the smallest number possible.
4. B
   Only three of the hoops are less than –5, i.e. –6, –7, –8.
5. E
   Each interval on the number line increases in steps of 25.
6. A
   Starting from 33, subtract in steps of 7 until you reach a number between 11 and 15.
7. D
8. C
   Each interval on the number line increases in steps of 0.02
9. A
   The '3' in the tens column rounds up to '4' because the value in the ones column is 5 or more.
10. B
    The attendance at Hardside City rounds to 24 000, whereas the others round to 25 000.
11. B
    The '3' in the tenths column rounds up to '4' because the value in the hundredths column is 5 or more.
12. D
    The temperatures should be ordered from the greatest positive value.
13. A
    The smallest number is –11 and the greatest is 17.

Pages 60–63
Practice Test 2: Calculations
1. C
   6 – (–4) = 10 as subtracting a negative number means you add it.
2. B
   400 ÷ 8 = 50
3. A
   23 × 57 = 1311
4. D
   Only options A and D have two prime numbers and, of these, only 11 and 7 sum to 18.
5. E
   5654 – 1287 = 4367
6. E
   Ava must now be 23 if she celebrated her 18th birthday five years ago.
7. E
   The ones digit of the two-digit number must be '6' since 6 × 4 = 24. Filling in the rest of the table shows that the multiplication is 134 × 56, which equals 7504.

8. D
   37 × 287 = 10 619
9. D
   25 – 64 = –39
10. A
    (23 × 15) + (5 × 5) = 370 people go to the theatre
    457 – 370 = 87 spare seats
11. B
    You can quickly see that A or B will give the smallest answer since they are multiplying the two smallest numbers (11 and 12). 11 × 12 + 13 – 14 = 131, whereas 12 × 11 + 14 – 13 = 133.
12. D
    755 + 700 = 1455
    1455 – 1230 = 225
13. B
    Following the rule of BIDMAS, the division (15 ÷ 3 = 5) must be done before the rest of the calculation.
    12 + 5 + 6 = 23.
14. E
    30 × £9 = £270; £345 – £270 = £75
    So 25 people paid an extra £3 for three courses (3 × £25).
15. B
    Clara makes 50p profit from each cup cake. 144 × £0.50 = £72
16. E
    $4^2 + \sqrt{16}$ and $5^2 - \sqrt{25}$ both equal 20.
17. A
    979 + 1037 = 2016
    2016 – 1862 = 154 are staff
    979 – 154 = 825 boys
18. D
    The lowest common multiple of 10 and 6 is 30, so 3 boxes of burgers and 5 packs of bread buns is the least number you can buy to have 30 of each.
19. A
    (2.07 + 4 + 3.1 + 8.83) = 18
    18 ÷ 3 = 6
20. C
    Completing, for example, the boxes in the top row (8) and the bottom row (11) means that the centre box must be 4 (23 – 11 – 8 = 4).
21. E
    Of the options, only 20 fulfils the criteria shown in the table.
22. D
    Options B and D are the only potential answers, since multiplying any number by 4 will give an even number and the other options are all odd. The answer must be 240 because it is a multiple of 4, whereas 230 is not.

Pages 64–67
Practice Test 3: Fractions, Decimals and Percentages
1. D
   48 ÷ 16 = 3, so 16 is $\frac{1}{3}$ of 48.
2. C
   In the second diagram, each of the three squares contains four equal parts so 12 in all. One part is shaded out of the total of 12.

3. A
   Convert mm to cm or cm to mm. Green makes up 8 cm of the 30 cm ribbon. A fraction of $\frac{8}{30}$ is $\frac{4}{15}$ in its simplest form.
4. B
   Convert the fractions to a common denominator of 24 in order to compare them.
5. D
   $\frac{3}{5}$ is the only option with both the numerator and denominator being prime numbers.
6. A
   Convert $\frac{1}{4}$ to $\frac{2}{8}$ in order to add it to $\frac{3}{8}$. $\frac{2}{8} + \frac{3}{8} = \frac{5}{8}$
7. E
   Claire spends £4 on the book and £15 on the jumper, so she has £5 left.
8. B
   270 ÷ 3 = 90, so this represents $\frac{1}{7}$ of the pupils in the school. Girls must represent $\frac{4}{7}$ of the pupils in the school, so 90 × 4 = 360 girls in the school.
9. D
   Three wholes are divided equally between five people, so each person gets $\frac{3}{5}$ = 0.6 = 60%.
10. B
    If £2.70 represents $\frac{2}{3}$, divide by 2 to find that £1.35 represents $\frac{1}{3}$. £1.35 × 3 = £4.05
11. E
    Three small buttons have the same width as two large buttons. The total width of two large buttons is 4.8 × 2 = 9.6 cm, so this is the width of three small buttons. So the diameter of one small button is 9.6 ÷ 3 = 3.2 cm.
12. B
    Making an estimate (2 × 4 = 8) shows that the only feasible answer is 8.64 among the possible options.
13. C
    (£0.87 × 2) + £0.56 + (£1.70 × 3) = £7.40
    £20 – £7.40 = £12.60
14. A
    12.8 ÷ 0.8 (or 1280 ÷ 80 if working in centimetres) = 16
15. D
    Compare the digits in each place value column.
16. E
    2.4 × 0.3 = (24 ÷ 10) × (3 ÷ 10) = 24 × 3 ÷ 10 ÷ 10 = 72 ÷ 100 = 0.72
17. E
    One half of each of the four segments is $\frac{1}{8}$ of the whole.
18. A
    If two rulers and five pencils cost £3.45 and two rulers and three pencils cost £2.75, the cost of two pencils is £3.45 – £2.75 = £0.70. So each pencil costs 35p. Three pencils would therefore cost £1.05 and subtracting

this from £2.75 leaves a £1.70 cost for two rulers. So each ruler costs £1.70 ÷ 2 = 85p.

19. E
Eight of the numbers (2, 3, 5, 11, 13, 17, 23, 29) out of 25 on the board are prime. $\frac{8}{25} = \frac{32}{100} = 32\%$

20. D
There are four red pens out of a total of 36 pens and pencils. $\frac{4}{36}$ is $\frac{1}{9}$ in its simplest form.

21. C
$0.6 + \frac{7}{10}$ sums to the same total as $\frac{3}{5} + 0.7$

22. A
$\frac{1}{3}$ off, i.e. £4 off the original price, is the best offer.

23. C
Six of the 14 shapes in the pattern are triangles. $\frac{6}{14}$ simplifies to $\frac{3}{7}$

24. B
If $\frac{1}{7}$ has been drunk by Dora, the remaining 300 ml represents $\frac{6}{7}$ of the original volume. 300 ÷ 6 = 50 ml. 50 ml is therefore $\frac{1}{7}$, so $\frac{7}{7}$ is 50 × 7 = 350 ml.

25. E

26. B
Karly spent 15 hours working on the project and Ahmed spent 16 hours.

27. B
8 chocolates represent 10% of the box. 80 – 32 = 48 chocolates are left, so these represent 60%.

Pages 68–71
Practice Test 4: Ratio and Proportion

1. C
$\frac{1}{5}$ of the Christmas bar will be removed to take it back to the original size. $\frac{1}{5} = 20\%$

2. A
Four DVDs would be 10% and two DVDs would be 5%. So 18 DVDs would be 9 lots of 5%, i.e. 45%

3. E
10% of 300 is 30, so 15% of 300 is 45. 300 – 45 = 255

4. B
If 24 girls represent 48% of the disco, each person at the disco represents 2% of the total. 52% are boys so there are 26 of them.

5. D
5% of £50 = £2.50. So she needs eight lots of £2.50 to increase her savings from £50 to £70.

6. C
10% of £4.80 is 48p, so 5% of £4.80 is 24p and 2.5% of £4.80 is 12p. £4.80 + £0.12 = £4.92

7. C
75 g would give $\frac{3}{4}$ of the amount of carbohydrate as 100 g. $\frac{3}{4}$ of 26.0 is 19.5

8. D
If there are 91 red beads, there are 13 lots of seven. Blue beads are in the same proportion: 13 × 4 = 52

9. A
The ratio has a total of 2 + 7 = 9 parts. So each part represents 36 ÷ 9 = 4 sweets. Orla gets seven parts of the ratio, so receives 7 × 4 = 28 sweets.

10. D
The ratio has a total of 2 + 3 = 5 parts. Juice is two of these parts, i.e. $\frac{2}{5}$.

11. E
40 cm of ribbon would cost $\frac{1}{3}$ of the price of 120 cm, i.e. 30p. 200 cm of ribbon would cost five times as much as 40 cm: 5 × 30p = 150p or £1.50

12. A
If it takes two men 6 days to build the wall, it would take one man 12 days. Three men would take $\frac{1}{3}$ of this time, i.e. 4 days.

13. D
In percentage terms, the ratio of raisins : chocolate drops : peanuts is 30 : 55 : 15. This simplifies to 6 : 11 : 3 if all parts of the ratio are divided by 5.

14. B
Increasing the sides of the rectangle by 25% takes the width to 5 cm and the length to 10 cm. 5 cm × 10 cm = 50 cm²

15. A
There are 7 + 5 = 12 parts in the ratio. One part represents 3600 ÷ 12 = 300 jewels. Princess Isabelle gets seven parts of the ratio: 7 × 300 = 2100

16. E
In centimetres, the ratio of red : white : blue is 45 : 30 : 25. This simplifies to 9 : 6 : 5 if all parts of the ratio are divided by 5.

17. B
(144 cm ÷ 6) × 8 = 192 cm

18. D
If Jodie has 93 hot dog sausages, she has multiplied the parts of the ratio by 31. So for sandwiches: 31 × 4 = 124

19. B
37 500 ÷ 50 = 750

20. A
575 × 8 = 4600

21. C
Four litres cost £6 so 28 litres cost seven times as much. £6 × 7 = £42

Pages 72–75
Practice Test 5: Algebra

1. E
The sequence decreases by 8 at each step.

2. D
The sequence increases by 3 at each step.

3. D
144 ÷ 16 = 9

4. C
$b = 9 + 15 = 24$

5. A
$d = 36 ÷ 4 = 9$, so $3d = 27$

6. D
The difference between consecutive numbers is 2, 3, 4, 5, 6.

7. C
The sequence increases by 4 at each step.

8. D
The sequence produced would be 4, 9, 16, 25, etc.

9. C
The lowest possible value of x is 77 and the greatest possible value of x is 83 in order for the statements to be true.

10. B
The four blocks weigh a total of 700 g – 400 g = 300 g. 300 g ÷ 4 = 75 g

11. A
Ben is 2 years younger than Bill, so Ben is $y – 2$ years old. So Alvin is $2(y – 2) = 2y – 4$ years old.

12. E
$2x + y = 48$ (y represents the side of the large square)
$x + y = 36$
Subtract these equations, so $x = 12$ cm, and as $12 + y = 36$, $y = 24$ cm

13. C
Use inverse operations, starting with Nazneen's output number.
27 + 1 = 28
28 ÷ 4 = 7
7 – 3 = 4

14. E
The cost of the pencils is multiplied by y and added to the cost of one pencil case.

15. D
The number of blocks in each shape increases by two at each step, so the missing shapes must have seven and nine blocks respectively.
3 + 5 + 7 + 9 + 11 = 35

16. E
$20 – 17 = 2m$
$2m = 3$, so $m = 3 ÷ 2 = 1.5$

17. C
Twenty-four batteries have been used over a period of 4 weeks.
So $4(p + q) = 24$, therefore $(p + q)$ must equal 6 and p must be greater than q since Josh uses more batteries. Therefore, $p = 4$, $q = 2$ is the only possible answer.

18. E
The sequence increases by £6 each week. The first multiple of 6 greater than 637 is 642, so Asad will have £5 left over after buying the bike.

19. B
The triangle has two longer sides of equal length and one shorter side. The perimeter is the total distance around the edge.

20. A
The possible combinations are: SR, SO, SC, SP, SB, RO, RC, RP, RB, OC, OP, OB, CP, CB, PB.

21. E
Continue the spiral in steps of 2 until you reach the shaded box.

Pages 76–81
Practice Test 6: Measurement
1. **C**
   15 minutes + 1 hour 55 minutes + 25 minutes = 2 hours 35 minutes
2. **A**
   A teaspoon would only hold about 5 ml, while the other options would hold much greater volumes than 40 ml.
3. **A**
   Fintan has grown by 18 cm, which equals 180 mm.
4. **D**
   November has 30 days, so December 1st will fall on Wednesday and December 4th on Saturday, which is exactly three weeks before the 25th.
5. **C**
   The scale shows Paula has bought 3.2 kg of onions.
   $3.2 \times 0.6 = 1.92$
6. **D**
   London is 9 hours behind 06.35, i.e. 21.35 the previous day.
7. **D**
   $36 \times 60 = 2160$ seconds, plus 0.25 of a minute, which is 15 seconds.
   $2160 + 15 = 2175$
8. **B**
   The original piece of card was $14 \text{ cm} \times 10 \text{ cm} = 140 \text{ cm}^2$
   Splitting the cross into three rectangles, its area is:
   $(6 \times 4) + (10 \times 6) + (4 \times 4) = 100 \text{ cm}^2$
   $140 \text{ cm}^2 - 100 \text{ cm}^2 = 40 \text{ cm}^2$
9. **A**
   $2 + 4 + 6 + 4 + 2 + 6 + 3 + 4 + 4 + 4 + 3 + 6 = 48$
10. **B**
    The arrival time in Los Angeles will be 3 hours and 5 minutes later than the departure time from London for a journey of 11 hours and 5 minutes.
    3.10 pm + 3 hours and 5 minutes = 6.15 pm.
11. **A**
    The length of the bedroom rounds to 5 m and the width to 4 m.
    $5 \text{ m} \times 4 \text{ m} = 20 \text{ m}^2$
12. **C**
    The surface area to be tiled is: $(6 \text{ m} \times 4 \text{ m}) + 2(6 \text{ m} \times 2.5 \text{ m}) + 2(4 \text{ m} \times 2.5 \text{ m}) = 74 \text{ m}^2$
    So three packs of tiles will be needed.
13. **E**
    The pieces shown sum to 5 cm + 1.7 cm + 3 cm = 9.7 cm.
    30 cm – 9.7 cm = 20.3 cm
14. **D**
    The heater has been left on for 15.5 hours.
    $15.5 \times £0.6 = £9.30$
15. **B**
    The volume of the box is $8 \text{ cm} \times 4 \text{ cm} \times 4 \text{ cm} = 128 \text{ cm}^3$
    The cubes are each $2 \text{ cm} \times 2 \text{ cm} \times 2 \text{ cm} = 8 \text{ cm}^3$
    $128 \div 8 = 16$
16. **B**
    Alice's letters weigh $6 \times 50 \text{ g} = 300 \text{ g}$
    Her parcels weigh $3 \times 750 \text{ g} = 2250 \text{ g}$
    $300 \text{ g} + 2250 \text{ g} = 2550 \text{ g}$ or 2.55 kg

17. **E**
    The area of the room is 3 m × 4 m = 12 m²
    The area occupied by the wardrobes is 2 m × 0.5 m = 1 m²
    12 m² – 1 m² = 11 m² to be carpeted.
18. **D**
    $5 \times 25 = 125$ minutes
    125 + 25 = 150 minutes (2 hours 30 minutes)
19. **A**
    The rectangle has a perimeter of $2(15.8 + 8.2) = 48 \text{ cm}$
    The square has a perimeter of 48 cm, so each side must be 12 cm.
    $12 \text{ cm} \times 12 \text{ cm} = 144 \text{ cm}^2$
20. **B**
    $200 \text{ cm} - (2 \times 62 \text{ cm}) = 76 \text{ cm}$
    $76 \text{ cm} \div 2 = 38 \text{ cm}$
21. **E**
    $11 - 19 + 5 = -3$
22. **A**
    2.25 litres = 2250 ml
    $2250 \div 250 = 9$
23. **C**
    Dimensions of 7 cm × 5 cm would give an area of 35 cm², not 24 cm².
24. **E**
    Suni spends a total of $(5 \times 0.2) + (4 \times 0.42) = £2.68$
    £20 – £2.68 = £17.32
    £17.32 ÷ 4 = £4.33
25. **B**
    $15 \times 12 = 180$
    $1260 \div 180 = 7$
26. **A**
    The total length of the edges is $(4 \times 12) + (4 \times 10) + (4 \times 30) = 208 \text{ cm}$
27. **B**
    $54 \times £12.75 = £688.50$
28. **C**
    John travels 32 km and Paul travels 30 miles (48 km).
    John travels 16 km less than Paul, which equals 10 miles.
29. **E**
    Area of the triangular face is $\frac{1}{2} (4 \text{ cm} \times 3 \text{ cm}) = 6 \text{ cm}^2$
    Volume is $6 \text{ cm}^2 \times 30 \text{ cm} = 180 \text{ cm}^3$
30. **C**
    Convert both measures to the same units:
    12 km = 12 000 m and 500 cm = 5 m
    $12 000 \div 5 = 2400$
31. **C**
    The volume not filled by water is $8 \text{ cm} \times 50 \text{ cm} \times 25 \text{ cm} = 10 000 \text{ cm}^3 = 10$ litres
    38 litres – 10 litres = 28 litres of water in the tank

Pages 82–87
Practice Test 7: Geometry
1. **D**
   Read the value on the x-axis first, then the value on the y-axis.
2. **A**
3. **B**
4. **A**
   The shaded angle in the square is 90°.
   The base angle of the isosceles triangle is $(180 - 80) \div 2 = 50°$.
   $90° + 50° = 140°$

5. **E**
   The angle opposite the marked 60° in the parallelogram is also 60°. There are two angles of this size at the point shared with the shaded angle. Angles at a point sum to 360°.
   The shaded angle is therefore $360° - (2 \times 60°) = 240°$
6. **C**
   A parallelogram has two pairs of equal sides.
7. **D**
   An isosceles triangle has one pair of equal sides.
8. **D**
   All the other options run into a mousetrap.
9. **E**
10. **E**
    When reflected, vertex O will be the same distance from the line $x = 4$ but on the other side of it.
11. **A**
    The shape moves -4 in the x direction and -3 in the y direction.
12. **C**
    Angles on a straight line sum to 180° so
    $5x = 180° - 80°$
    $x = 20°$
13. **D**
    Angle $x = 540° \div 5 = 108°$
    Angle $y = 360° - 108° = 252°$
14. **B**
    Since the length of the rectangle is six squares, the width will be three squares.
15. **D**
    The x co-ordinate of the midpoint will be halfway between the x co-ordinates of points P and Q. The y co-ordinate of the midpoint will be halfway between the y co-ordinates.
16. **B**
    B is the only option in which the x and y co-ordinates of the new end points change by equal values (they each increase by +1).
17. **C**
    At four o'clock, the long hand is pointing at 12 and the smaller hour hand is one-third of the way around the clock. One-third of 360° = 120°.
18. **D**
19. **D**
    A rhombus has four equal sides; none of the other options are properties of a rhombus.
20. **E**
21. **C**
    The front view of the building will be the exact reflection of the rear view.
22. **D**
    The lake is in the North-East, so a 180° turn means the bridge is in the South-West.
23. **B**
    The first turn has to be L, so this rules out C. A and E don't reach square F. D does reach the square but goes over an oil patch. This leaves B.

Pages 88–93
Practice Test 8: Statistics
1. **E**
These are the only two pairs on the chart which have the same distance (98 miles).
2. **E**
8 pupils scored 0–20 marks but only 4 scored 81–100 marks.
3. **C**
Adding up the values for January to June inclusive: 3 + 4 + 2 + 3 + 8 + 10 = 30
4. **E**
23 – 11 = 12 girls are over 14. There are 27 girls in total: 27 – 12 – 8 = 7 are aged 10–14.
5. **B**
(32 + 29 + 28 + 35) ÷ 4 = 31
6. **A**
Anji improved in Science by 5 marks (from 2 to 7), which was a greater increase than in any other subject.
7. **A**
The segment for 'The Superheroes' is 60°, which is $\frac{1}{6}$ of the whole of the chart. So 36 × 6 = 216 people were surveyed altogether.
8. **C**
Add up the numbers in the circles for science fiction (3) and comedy (1), and in the overlap which doesn't include romance (1).
9. **B**
Find 5.5 on the kilograms axis and read up to the line. Then read across to the vertical axis to find the equivalent value in pounds.
10. **D**
The pie chart is split into 12 equal segments. Salt and vinegar occupies five of the 12 segments, which is more than $\frac{1}{3}$.
11. **D**
More than 5 bicycles were sold on Tuesday (6), Friday (6), Saturday (10) and Sunday (8).
12. **A**
Sixty children were surveyed and there are 12 shaded blocks on the chart, so each shaded block represents five children. Football is the only sport with three shaded blocks (5 × 3 = 15).
13. **C**
An equilateral triangle has no parallel sides and has three equal angles of 60°.
14. **B**
20 – (4 + 5 + 2) = 9 chose purple.
15. **B**
If the mean of the five exam results is 56, then the total marks scored across all the exams was 5 × 56 = 280.
280 – 40 – 56 – 70 – 66 = 48
16. **B**
The temperature at 9am was 8°C and at 3pm was 20°C, so an increase of 12 degrees.
17. **A**
(5y + 3) + (7y + 4) + (3y – 1) = 15y + 6
(15y + 6) ÷ 3 = 5y + 2
18. **E**
$\frac{1}{5}$ = 20% so read off the graph at 20%.

Pages 95–106: Practice Paper 1
1. **C**
The number shown is thirty-two thousand, seven hundred and fifty, so the 7 is in the 'hundreds' place.
2. **B**
Three 40 cm pieces add up to 120 cm, so 10 cm are left over.
3. **A**
Each cone represents 20 people. Chocolate shows 4.5 cones and vanilla shows 3 cones. There is a difference of 1.5 cones.
1.5 × 20 = 30
4. **D**
The interior angles of any quadrilateral sum to 360°.
360° – (100° + 60° + 80°) = 120°
5. **E**
The height of each bar shows the number of children. 9 said Ham and Cheese, 8 said BLT and 3 said Prawn Mayonnaise.
9 + 8 + 3 = 20
6. **A**
3 cm is 0.03 m.
1.54 m + 0.03 m = 1.57 m
7. **D**
The net will fold up to have 2 hexagonal faces and 6 rectangular faces so it is a hexagonal prism.
8. **A**
The proportion of each section on the pie chart represents the proportion of 120 children that said each category.
$\frac{45}{360}$ × 120 = 15 children said non-fiction.
120 – 15 = 105 children said either adventure, science fiction or mystery.
9. **C**
1 kg is 1000 g.
1000 g – 850 g = 150 g.
To convert g to kg, divide by 1000.
150 ÷ 1000 = 0.15
10. **D**
Start at 4 weeks on the x-axis, follow that up to the line and read across to 1.2 kg on the y-axis.
11. **C**
Find 15% of £25. 10% is £2.50 and 5% is £1.25.
£2.50 + £1.25 = £3.75
12. **E**
Ava is walking the fastest where the gradient of the line is the steepest.
13. **B**
Substitute 9 into the formula.
C = 5 + 2(9 – 1) = 21
14. **E**
The village hall is at 2 on the horizontal (x-axis) and 7 on the vertical (y-axis).
15. **C**
Point A is three units to the left of the mirror line in the x-direction, so the reflection will be three units to the right of the mirror line. The y-direction remains unchanged.
16. **A**
The radius is half the diameter. 2 × 15 = 30 cm.
17. **C**
To find the mean, add up the values and divide by the number of values.
(13 + 17 + 20 + 14 + 16) ÷ 5 = 16
18. **A**
Find $\frac{1}{4}$ of 84 first.
84 ÷ 4 = 21, then $\frac{3}{4}$ of 84 is 21 × 3 = 63
19. **B**
To convert litres to millilitres, multiply by 1000.
0.75 × 1000 = 750
The bucket will hold 1250 – 750 = 500 ml more.
20. **D**
Point X is at 3 on the horizontal (x-axis) and 2 on the vertical (y-axis).
21. **D**
The highest bar is Lollies.
22. **B**
Use equivalent fractions to order the fractions from smallest to greatest.
$\frac{1}{2} = \frac{4}{8}$ and $\frac{3}{4} = \frac{6}{8}$
Then order by the numerators.
23. **A**
48 minutes later than 11.15 is 12.03.
24. **D**
The perimeter is 1 + 1 + 1.5 + 1.5 = 5 m
25. **E**
The train leaves at 16.51 and arrives at 17.55, a difference of 64 minutes.
26. **B**
Look at the height of the bars of broccoli, green beans and peas.
6 + 4 + 8 = 18
27. **D**
18 is both an even number and a multiple of 3.
28. **B**
18 ÷ 1.5 = 12, so it will take her 12 weeks.
29. **C**
2 squares will fit vertically and 3 horizontally so 6 squares will fit in the rectangle.
30. **E**
18.5 – 2 = 16.5
31. **A**
The perimeter of the frame is 2 × (75 + 40) = 230 cm
32. **C**
The graph shows the population in 1990 was 5 billion. Find 2.5 billion on the y-axis, follow over to the graph and follow down to the x-axis to see the year 1950.
33. **C**
Look at the given calculation and compare the answers.
18.9 is 1890 ÷ 100.
So the missing number in the second calculation is 3 ÷ 100 = 0.03.
34. **E**
Add up the height of the bars.
6 + 8 + 10 + 6 + 12 = 42
35. **A**
Use a common denominator of 16.
$\frac{3}{8} = \frac{6}{16}$, so $\frac{15}{16} - \frac{6}{16} = \frac{9}{16}$
36. **A**
If each side increases by a factor of 3, the volume increases by a factor of 3^3 = 27.

37. **E**
    £2.50 × 15 = £37.50
38. **B**
    The angle is a reflex angle. It is greater than 180° and smaller than 360°.
39. **C**
    £360 ÷ 3 = £120
40. **B**
    562 × 7 = 3934
41. **D**
    Angles on a straight line add up to 180°.
    180° − 108° = 72°
42. **B**
    There are 14 blocks used in the bar chart.
    140 children were surveyed. Each block represents 140 ÷ 14 = 10 children.
    Summer shows 5 blocks: 5 × 10 = 50
43. **E**
    Compare the net to the cuboid. The height is 3 cm.
44. **C**
    Change £ to pence by multiplying by 100.
    £20 is 2000p, then 20 ÷ 2000 = 0.01 = 1%
45. **D**
    Speed = Distance ÷ Time
    120 miles ÷ 3 hours = 40 miles per hour
46. **E**
    Shape 3 is a reflection of Shape 2. It is the same shape just reflected over a mirror line.
47. **D**
    180 ÷ 15 = 12, so the missing number is 12.
48. **C**
    The time difference between 12.14 and 10.50 is one hour and 24 minutes, or 84 minutes.
49. **A**
    Since the mean after 4 tests was 20, she scored a total of 4 × 20 = 80.
    The mean after 5 tests was 21, so she scored a total of 5 × 21 = 105.
    105 − 80 = 25
50. **B**
    $(x − 3, y − 4)$ and $(x + 3, y − 4)$ are both 3 units in the x-direction and 4 units in the y-direction from (x, y) so the shape is an isosceles triangle.

Pages 107–120: Practice Paper 2

1. **A**
    There are four tick marks between each integer, so each tick mark is 0.2. The arrow points to 12.4.
2. **C**
    7.5 + 3 = 10.5
3. **A**
    7095 has 7 in the thousands place, 0 in the hundreds, 9 in the tens and 5 in the ones place.
4. **B**
    The height of the bars is misleading. 30% is shown to be almost as high as 50% and 20% is well below half of the height of the 50% bar.
5. **C**
    Shapes 2, 3 and 5 are all pentagons but Shape 3 is the only regular pentagon because the angles in the pentagon are all equal and the side lengths are all equal.
6. **D**
    (50 + 45 + 45 + 42 + 43) ÷ 5 = 45
7. **E**
    Kieran is currently 13 − 3 = 10 years old. Lilly is half as old as Kieran. Lilly is 5.
8. **C**
    Three-quarters of an hour is 45 minutes and 45 minutes before 8.50 am is 8.05 am.
9. **A**
    30 × 50 ml = 1500 ml. To convert ml to l, divide by 1000. 1500 ml = 1.5 l
10. **C**
    Angles in a triangle add to 180°. All three angles in an equilateral triangle are equal. 180° ÷ 3 = 60°
11. **B**
    The sequence is going up in 5s.
    −1 + 5 = 4
12. **C**
    The bar for Chevelle is the highest.
13. **A**
    Pints are on the x-axis so read up from 7 on the x-axis to meet the line. Then read across to the y-axis. 7 pints is approximately 4 litres.
14. **E**
    Multiplying 56 × 99 is the same as multiplying 56 × 100 and subtracting 56.
15. **D**
    Each circle represents 10 children. There are 17.5 circles. 17.5 × 10 = 175
16. **E**
    162 ÷ 9 = 18
17. **D**
    Follow the path through the map. Be careful not to mix up left and right turns.
18. **A**
    75 minutes is 1 hour and 15 minutes. 16.15 is 4.15 pm. 1 hour and 15 minutes before is 3.00 pm.
19. **C**
    8 is both a multiple of 4 and a factor of 72.
20. **D**
    Distance = Speed × Time.
    740 × 8.5 = 6290. An easier way to do this calculation without a calculator is to multiply 740 × 8 = 5920, then add half of 740:
    740 ÷ 2 = 370
    5920 + 370 = 6290
21. **E**
    Use the common denominator 9.
    $\frac{1}{3} = \frac{3}{9}$, so $\frac{1}{3} + \frac{4}{9} = \frac{3}{9} + \frac{4}{9} = \frac{7}{9}$
22. **D**
    Read up from Month 3 on the x-axis to the curve, then follow over to approximately 5 million on the y-axis. Read across from 10 million on the y-axis to the curve then down to Month 5 on the x-axis.
23. **A**
    250 g is 2.5 × 100 g
    2.5 × £0.30 = £0.75
24. **D**
    Everything will be reversed left-to-right in the view from the rear of the building.
25. **B**
    To find 10%, divide by 10. 40 ÷ 10 = 4. To find 70%, multiply 4 × 7 = 28.
26. **D**
    The only reasonable measurement for the height of a door is 2.1 m.
27. **E**
    Convert all the numbers to be in the same form. As decimals:
    68% = 0.68, 6.8% = 0.068, $\frac{6}{8} = \frac{3}{4} = 0.75$
    0.75 is the greatest.
28. **C**
    The diameter is the distance across the circle through the centre. The distance from the centre to the circumference is half the diameter.
    24 cm ÷ 2 = 12 cm
29. **B**
    3.2 + 3.2 + 3.8 + 3 = 13.2
30. **B**
    5 smaller rectangles will fit along the length and 5 along the width of the larger rectangle so 25 rectangles will fit.
31. **E**
    The x co-ordinate of point Z is 7 units away from the y-axis, so the reflection will be 7 units away from the y-axis. The y co-ordinate will stay the same. Point Z will be (7, −4).
32. **B**
    She buys three pairs of socks.
    3 × £2.20 = £6.60, then £7.20 + £18.50 + £6.60 + £20.00 = £52.30
33. **B**
    First find the missing value in the top row: 50 − (20 + 17) = 13.
    Then find the centre of the middle row using the values from the middle column:
    50 − (13 + 21) = 16.
    Then the missing value is
    50 − (19 + 16) = 15.
34. **D**
    The sequence is going up in 4 sticks. The third picture has 21 sticks so the fifth has 21 + 4 + 4 = 29 sticks.
35. **E**
    Use the common denominator of 8.
    $\frac{3}{4} = \frac{6}{8}$, $\frac{1}{2} = \frac{4}{8}$, $\frac{4}{16} = \frac{2}{8}$ then compare the fractions.
36. **B**
    The volume of the sand pit is
    2 m × 3 m × 0.5 m = 3 m³.
    The sand is sold in 0.3 m³ boxes, so
    3 m³ ÷ 0.3 m³ = 10
37. **D**
    Each side increasing by a factor of 10 means the volume increases by a factor of 10 × 10 × 10 = 1000.
38. **C**
    720 children were surveyed so each degree of the circle represents 2 children.
    2 × 210 = 420 children said fish and chips.
    2 × 60 = 120 children said roast dinner.
    300 more children said fish and chips than said roast dinner.

39. E
Work out the co-ordinates of point
L shown here. Point L is on the x-axis
and is –1 away from the y-axis, (–1, 0).
Then point M must be (–1, 4) because
the distance from (1, –4) to the x-axis
is 4. Point N has the same y value as
point M and is 4 units larger in the x
direction. Point N must be (3, 4).

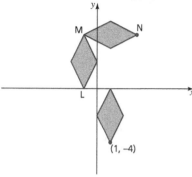

40. D
All the answers are whole numbers,
so you only need to look at whole
number side lengths.
The factor pairs of 36 are: 1 × 36,
2 × 18, 3 × 12, and 4 × 9.
The possible perimeters are therefore
2 × (1 cm + 36 cm) = 74 cm,
2 × (2 cm + 18 cm) = 40 cm, and so on.
2 × (3 cm + 12 cm) = 30 cm

41. C
The shape has 12 + 30 + 20 = 62 faces
and 60 vertices.
Substitute into V – E + F = 2,
60 – E + 62 = 2 to find E = 120.

42. E
The mean of the weekdays is
(30 + 40 + 20 + 40 + 60) ÷ 5 = 38.
The mean of the weekend is
(100 + 110) ÷ 2 = 105.
105 – 38 = 67

43. B
A trapezium has two sides parallel and
the sides are not all equal.

44. B
Each board plus a divider is
50 cm + 5 cm = 55 cm. There will be one
extra divider at the end so subtract
that end from the total. 2.8 m = 280 cm
and 280 – 5 = 275. 275 ÷ 55 = 5, so 5
boards and 6 dividers are needed.

45. D
The angles add up to 360°.
3x + x + 3x + x = 8x and 360 ÷ 8 = 45
so x = 45°.
Then 3x = 3 × 45° = 135°.

46. A
There are 30 – (12 + 10) = 8 children in
Giraffe class who said dodgeball. Then
there are 20 – 8 = 12 children in Zebra
Class who said their favourite was
dodgeball.

47. D
The carton holds 15 × 5 × 10 = 750 cm³
of sugar cubes, so 750 cubes.
750 × 2.3 g = 1725 g, which is 1.725 kg.

48. E
The line of symmetry shows where the
shape would be the same if you folded
along the line. Shape 5 would be the
same if you folded it along the line of
symmetry.

49. C
Pink and purple make up 120° of
the pie chart and 60 people, so 2°
represents one person. She surveyed
360 ÷ 2 = 180 people.

50. A
The mean after five runs is 41 seconds
so the total time of the first five runs is
5 × 41 = 205 seconds.
The mean after the sixth run is 40
seconds, so the total time after 6 runs
is 6 × 40 = 240 seconds.
His sixth run is 240 – 205 = 35 seconds.

Pages 121–136: Practice Paper 3
1. E
Twenty thousand five hundred and
thirteen has 2 in the ten thousands
place, 5 in the hundreds place, 1 in the
tens place and 3 in the ones place, i.e.
20 513

2. C
Salt and Vinegar has 1.5 more packets
than Cheese and Onion. Each packet is
18 people.
18 × 1.5 = 27 people

3. B
7.327 metres is 732.7 cm. Rounded to
the nearest cm this is 733 cm.

4. B
The angle is less than 90° so it is an
acute angle.

5. D
5 × 500 g = 2500 g.
To convert g to kg, divide by 1000.
2500 g = 2.5 kg

6. B
A hexagon has six sides and Shape 2
has five sides.

7. A
552 × 2 = 1104, so 1104 × 35 =
19 320 × 2 = 38 640.

8. D
(10 + 12 + 9 + 8 + 11) ÷ 5 = 10

9. E
30 × 125 ml = 3750 ml. To convert
millilitres to litres, divide by 1000.
3750 ml = 3.75 litres

10. C
The sequence is going down in 6s.
518 – 6 = 512

11. C
The gradient is the least between 4
months and 5 months.

12. E
12 cm × 2 cm × 3 cm = 72 cm³

13. A
Add up the height of each bar.
6 + 10 + 4 + 8 = 28

14. E
Dividing by 100 moves the digits two
places to the right.
397 ÷ 100 = 3.97

15. C
The biggest section of the pie chart is
Chocolates.

16. C
The point is at –2 on the x-axis and 4
on the y-axis.

17. C
The sunflowers grew 10 cm from Week
3 to Week 4, more than any other
week.

18. A
75 minutes is 1 hour and 15 minutes.
1 hour and 15 minutes before 3.30 pm
is 2.15 pm, which is 14.15 in 24-hour
format.

19. D
20 children preferred bananas, 10
preferred apples and 5 preferred
grapes.
20 + 10 – 5 = 25

20. E
Convert each number to a percentage
and then order from smallest to
largest.
$\frac{1}{20}$ = 5%, $\frac{3}{50}$ = 6% and 0.36 = 36%

21. A
Use equivalent fractions to convert $\frac{1}{8}$
into $\frac{2}{16}$.
$\frac{13}{16} - \frac{2}{16} = \frac{11}{16}$

22. B
A three-quarter clockwise turn from
due East is North. The school is North
of where he is standing.

23. B
The train leaves Birmingham at 20.08
and arrives at Warwick at 20.26. The
journey lasts 18 minutes.

24. E
Split 42 into the ratio 2 : 1.
42 ÷ 3 = 14 and 14 × 2 = 28

25. B
Angles in a quadrilateral add up to
360°.
360° – (110° + 80° + 40°) = 130°

26. A
First find the number of boys with
green eyes: 12 – 7 = 5
Then add up the number of boys:
2 + 5 + 8 = 15

27. A
(43 × 817) + (57 × 817) = 100 × 817 =
81 700

28. E
There are 10 blocks shaded in total.
100 people were surveyed so each
block is 100 ÷ 10 = 10 people.
The bar that represents Walk has 5
blocks: 5 × 10 = 50

29. B
It costs 2 × £23 = £46 for one adult.
4 children's tickets cost 4 × £23 = £92
2 adult tickets cost 2 × £46 = £92
4 children and 2 adult tickets cost
£92 + £92 = £184

30. D
A pyramid meets at a point. Net D
folds up to meet at a point and has a
triangular base.

31. A
Convert £16.00 to pence.
1600 ÷ 20 = 80

32. C

$\frac{1}{4} = 0.25$ so multiply by 0.25

33. B

There are 2000 rabbits in July and 900 in May.
2000 − 900 = 1100

34. B

He spends £2.20 + £1.20 + £2.00 + £1.30
= £6.70
£10.00 − £6.70 = £3.30

35. A

The proportion of the pie chart is the proportion of the birds.
She sees $24 \times \frac{60}{360} = 4$ sparrows and $24 \times \frac{30}{360} = 2$ parakeets

36. C

The thermometer shows 12°C.
12°C − 15°C = −3°C

37. D

Speed = Distance ÷ Time
180 ÷ 3 = 60 mph

38. A

Point X is 4 units above the x-axis, so the reflection will be 4 units below the x-axis, (1, −4)

39. D

The mean is the total divided by the number of items. The total must be 20 if the mean is 5 because 20 ÷ 4 = 5.
5 + 6 + 3 = 14, so Year 5 must be 6.

40. E

Ingrid is 18, so Henry is 21. James is twice as old as Henry, 42.

41. C

Split the kitchen into a 3 m × 1 m rectangle and a 1 m × 1 m square.

42. C

Start at 77 and go down in 8s until the sequence reaches a number between 50 and 60.
77, 69, 61, 53
She must have started at 53.

43. D

Angles in a triangle add to 180°.
180° − (43° + 32°) = 105°

44. C

One quarter of an hour is 15 minutes.
15 minutes before 15.40 is 15.25, or 3.25 pm.

45. D

A line of symmetry splits a shape into two sides that are exactly the same.
Shape 3 and Shape 4 do not have a line of symmetry.

46. E

Point X is at (−6, 5). Moving 4 units to the right and 2 units down moves it to (−2, 3).

47. A

To mentally divide 42 ÷ 3.5, first divide 42 ÷ 7 = 6, then multiply 6 × 2 = 12.

48. C

Read up from 25 miles on the x-axis to meet the line, then read across to 40 km on the y-axis.

49. D

There are 4 + 13 = 17 children less than 130 cm.
50 children were measured.
$\frac{17}{50} = 34\%$

50. B

Angles in a triangle add to 180°.
The missing angle in the triangle is:
180° − (40° + 45°) = 95°
Angles on a straight line add to 180°.
180° − (50° + 95°) = 35°

Pages 137–149: Practice Paper 4

1. C

The 2 is in the thousands place.

2. B

Each star represents 6 people. There are 1.5 more stars for Dr Dark than for Amazing A.
1.5 × 6 = 9

3. D

The interior angles of any quadrilateral sum to 360°.

4. B

5% is 0.05. £5.00 × 0.05 = £0.25
Alternatively, find half of 10% of £5.00.

5. C

The digits have moved three places to the right, which is the same as dividing by 1000.

6. B

Vertically opposite angles are the same.

7. B

None of the numbers are prime numbers. 14 is not a multiple of 3. 75 is not even. 114 is not a two-digit number. The only option that applies to all the numbers is B.

8. C

If the fountain is on her right and the school is in front of her, she is facing West.

9. E

$\frac{1}{4} \times 50 = 12.5$

All the others give an answer of 37.50

10. B

A line of symmetry is a mirror line. The shape will be a trapezium when it is reflected over the line.

11. A

To convert litres to ml, multiply by 1000.
1.2 litres = 1200 ml.
He can fill 1200 ÷ 80 = 15 pots.

12. B

The scale on the x-axis is uneven. The space between 2000 and 2020 spans 20 years but is the same size as 1980 to 1990 and 1990 to 2000.

13. E

The flat part of the graph shows when she would have been at a friend's house. The graph shows a varying gradient heading towards and away from the friend's house. The graph starts and ends at a distance of zero, so she goes home after visiting her friend.

14. A

He should round 27p to 30p and needs to remember to not mix up pence and pounds in the calculation.

15. D

The height of the bars shows the number of children.
125 children said dolls, 150 said cars and 75 said building bricks.
125 + 150 − 75 = 200

16. B

If there are three times as many girls as boys, then $\frac{1}{4}$ of the class are boys.
There are 28 ÷ 4 = 7 boys so there are 3 × 7 = 21 girls.

17. E

The analogue clock shows the time 6.23pm. 17.51 is 5.51pm.
The difference between the two times is 32 minutes.

18. C

In total Year 5 has read 95 + 75 + 85 = 255 books so they need to read 300 − 255 = 45 more books.

19. C

Best solved in a grid, remembering that sausage and onion is the same as onion and sausage, etc.
6 + 5 + 4 + 3 + 2 + 1 = 21 options.

20. C

To find the mean, add up the values and divide by the number of values.
(12 + 14 + 11 + 11) ÷ 4 = 12

21. A

9 hours is 9 × 60 × 60 = 32 400 seconds.
56 minutes is 56 × 60 = 3360 seconds.
32 400 + 3360 = 35 760

22. C

Each circle represents 12 children.
4 × 12 = 48 children said 'hip hop',
6.5 × 12 = 78 children said 'pop' and
3 × 12 = 36 said 'classical'.
(48 + 78 − 36) = 90 more children said 'hip hop' or 'pop' than said 'classical'.

23. D

Point X is at (−6, −1). A translation of 7 units right moves the x co-ordinate to 1. A translation of 3 units up moves the y co-ordinate to 2.

24. C

36 is 1.5 × 24, so the measurements need to be multiplied by 1.5.
250 × 1.5 = 375

25. D

3.6 metres is 3600 mm. He will need 3600 ÷ 200 = 18 bricks for each row across the drive. 4.8 metres is 4800 mm. He will need 4800 ÷ 100 = 48 rows. He needs 18 × 48 = 864 bricks.

26. E

£1 + £0.50 + (5 × £0.05) + (2 × £0.01) = £1.77

27. A

Use inverse operations: 5 × 15 = 75, so 75 ÷ 15 = 5.

28. E

Pie charts show the proportion, not the actual raw data, so the only thing that can be compared is the proportion of trains.

29. D

Count up in 6s from 45 to arrive at 63.

30. B
A heptagonal pyramid has seven faces around the sides and one for the base.

31. E
80 mm is 8 cm. There are eight faces that are 20 cm by 8 cm.
The total area is then $8 \times 8\,cm \times 20\,cm$ $= 1280\,cm^2$.

32. D
Convert each measurement to metres first by dividing by 100.
$0.6 \times 0.2 \times 0.5 = 0.06\,m^3$

33. A
The middle space on the bottom row is $27 - (8 + 6) = 13$.
The middle space of the middle row is then $27 - (5 + 13) = 9$.
The space with the star is $27 - (9 + 11)$ $= 7$.

34. D
Don't forget to line up the digits by place value.

35. C
Find the lowest common multiple of 6 and 8.
Four packs of hot dogs is $4 \times 6 = 24$ hot dogs and 3 packs of buns is $3 \times 8 = 24$ buns.

36. D
£110 − £45 = £65 and $65 \div 15$ is between 4 and 5, so she needs to save for 5 months.

37. D
Look at the shape as a large trapezium instead of a shape made of smaller shapes. The base angle of the large trapezium is 60° because it is an equilateral triangle. The top angle of the large trapezium is then 120° so the missing angle is 360° − 120° = 240°.

38. D
Each cake makes a profit of 50p − 15p = 35p.
$200 \times £0.35 = £70$

39. E
Quarter to 4 means 3.45pm, or 15.45. The programme finishes at 16.27 so it is 42 minutes long.

40. C
Follow the path through the map. Be careful not to mix up left and right turns.

41. E
He has $\frac{1}{3} \times 48 = 16$ stamps and $48 - 16$ $= 32$ left to collect.

42. A
Convert both measurements to cm.
4 feet is $4 \times 12 = 48$ inches, so 4 feet and 10 inches is 58 inches, which is approximately $58 \times 2.5 = 145\,cm$. 1.53 m is 153 cm. Naseem is approximately $153 - 145 = 8\,cm$ taller.

43. C
The area to be covered is $(3\,m \times 6\,m) -$ $(1\,m \times 4\,m) = 14\,m^2$. Each roll of turf covers $0.5\,m^2$ so she will need 28 rolls. A good estimate is $28 \times £3 = £84$

44. A
The cost is shown as £5 plus £0.15 multiplied by the number of miles.

45. B
In section 4 of the graph he has driven 40 miles (from 55 miles to 95 miles) in 40 minutes (90 to 130 minutes), which is a speed of 60 mph. In section 5 of the graph he has driven 15 miles (95 miles to 110 miles) in 30 minutes (130 to 160 minutes), which is a speed of 30 mph.

46. E
2 litres is 2000 ml. Split 2000 ml into five parts (because there are four parts white paint and one part red paint): 2000 ml ÷ 5 = 400 ml. Each part is 400 ml and there are four parts white paint, so you need $4 \times 400\,ml = 1600\,ml$ of white paint.

47. E
The drinks total is
£88.20 − (£9.80 + £62.40) = £16.00.
Each drink is £3.20 and 16 ÷ 3.20 = 5.

48. B
Opposite angles in a parallelogram are the same and angles in a quadrilateral sum to 360°, so the angle inside the parallelogram on the line is 100°. Angles on a line sum to 180° so the missing angle is 180° − (50° + 100°) = 30°.

49. A
A pallet box holds $20 \times 9 = 180$ rolls of toilet roll. Without a calculator, you can see that 3700 ÷ 180 is between 20 and 21 ($180 \times 20 = 3600$) so 21 pallet boxes are needed.

50. B
The point $(a, 5)$ and $(a + 2, 5)$ have the same y co-ordinate so they form a straight horizontal line. $(a - 2, 0)$ and $(a + 2, 0)$ also have the same y co-ordinate so they also form a straight horizontal line. The point $(a + 2, 0)$ and $(a + 2, 5)$ have the same x co-ordinate so they form a straight vertical line. The point $(a, 5)$ and $(a - 2, 0)$ do not share an x or y co-ordinate so they form a slanted line. The shape made by two parallel lines and two non-parallel lines is a trapezium. It can help to sketch the points. Choose a value for a and plot the points.

Progress Charts

Track your progress by shading in your score at each attempt.

Practice Papers

	Date:	Attempt 1	Practice Paper 1
Score /50			
Score /50	Date:	Attempt 2	

	Date:	Attempt 1	Practice Paper 2
Score /50			
Score /50	Date:	Attempt 2	

	Date:	Attempt 1	Practice Paper 3
Score /50			
Score: /50	Date:	Attempt 2	

	Date:	Attempt 1	Practice Paper 4
Score /50			
Score /50	Date:	Attempt 2	

Practice Tests

	Score	Date:	Attempt 1	Practice Test 1: Number and Place Value
/13				
/13	Score	Date:	Attempt 2	

	Score	Date:	Attempt 1	Practice Test 2: Calculations
/22				
/22	Score	Date:	Attempt 2	

	Score	Date:	Attempt 1	Practice Test 3: Fractions, Decimals and Percentages
/27				
/27	Score	Date:	Attempt 2	

	Score	Date:	Attempt 1	Practice Test 4: Ratio and Proportion
/21				
/21	Score	Date:	Attempt 2	

	Score	Date:	Attempt 1	Practice Test 5: Algebra
/21				
/21	Score	Date:	Attempt 2	

	Score	Date:	Attempt 1	Practice Test 6: Measurement
/31				
/31	Score	Date:	Attempt 2	

	Score	Date:	Attempt 1	Practice Test 7: Geometry
/23				
/23	Score	Date:	Attempt 2	

	Score	Date:	Attempt 1	Practice Test 8: Statistics
/18				
/18	Score	Date:	Attempt 2	

MATHS PRACTICE PAPER 1

Pupil's Name

School Name

Date of Test

DATE OF BIRTH

Day	Month	Year
[0] [0]	January ▭	2007 ▭
[1] [1]	February ▭	2008 ▭
[2] [2]	March ▭	2009 ▭
[3] [3]	April ▭	2010 ▭
[4]	May ▭	2011 ▭
[5]	June ▭	2012 ▭
[6]	July ▭	2013 ▭
[7]	August ▭	2014 ▭
[8]	September ▭	2015 ▭
[9]	October ▭	2016 ▭
	November ▭	2017 ▭
	December ▭	2018 ▭

PUPIL NUMBER

[0] [0] [0] [0] [0] [0]
[1] [1] [1] [1] [1] [1]
[2] [2] [2] [2] [2] [2]
[3] [3] [3] [3] [3] [3]
[4] [4] [4] [4] [4] [4]
[5] [5] [5] [5] [5] [5]
[6] [6] [6] [6] [6] [6]
[7] [7] [7] [7] [7] [7]
[8] [8] [8] [8] [8] [8]
[9] [9] [9] [9] [9] [9]

SCHOOL NUMBER

[0] [0] [0] [0] [0] [0] [0]
[1] [1] [1] [1] [1] [1] [1]
[2] [2] [2] [2] [2] [2] [2]
[3] [3] [3] [3] [3] [3] [3]
[4] [4] [4] [4] [4] [4] [4]
[5] [5] [5] [5] [5] [5] [5]
[6] [6] [6] [6] [6] [6] [6]
[7] [7] [7] [7] [7] [7] [7]
[8] [8] [8] [8] [8] [8] [8]
[9] [9] [9] [9] [9] [9] [9]

Please mark like this ⊟.

1
7 ones ▭
7 tens ▭
7 hundreds ▭
7 thousands ▭
7 ten thousands ▭

2
5 cm ▭
10 cm ▭
15 cm ▭
20 cm ▭
25 cm ▭

3
30 people ▭
5 people ▭
10 people ▭
15 people ▭
25 people ▭

4
110° ▭
100° ▭
60° ▭
120° ▭
80° ▭

5
12 children ▭
14 children ▭
4 children ▭
24 children ▭
20 children ▭

6
1.57 m ▭
15.43 m ▭
157 m ▭
0.157 m ▭
1.543 m ▭

7
A ▭
B ▭
C ▭
D ▭
E ▭

8
105 children ▭
100 children ▭
90 children ▭
80 children ▭
75 children ▭

9
1.5 kg ▭
15 g ▭
0.15 kg ▭
0.015 kg ▭
1.05 g ▭

10
1.02 kg ▭
1.0 kg ▭
1.4 kg ▭
1.2 kg ▭
1.1 kg ▭

11
£10.00 ▭
£15.00 ▭
£3.75 ▭
£2.50 ▭
£5.00 ▭

12
Section 1 ▭
Section 2 ▭
Section 3 ▭
Section 4 ▭
Section 5 ▭

13
£9.00 ▭
£21.00 ▭
£16.00 ▭
£5.00 ▭
£14.00 ▭

14
(2, 1) ▭
(7, 2) ▭
(1, 2) ▭
(8, 5) ▭
(2, 7) ▭

15
(5, 8) ▭
(5, 9) ▭
(8, 5) ▭
(7, 5) ▭
(8, 9) ▭

16
30 cm ▭
25 cm ▭
15 cm ▭
20 cm ▭
7.5 cm ▭

17
20 ▭
12 ▭
16 ▭
17 ▭
10 ▭

18
63 ▭
21 ▭
42 ▭
11 ▭
8 ▭

19
0.25 l ▭
500 ml ▭
450 ml ▭
0.75 l ▭
350 ml ▭

20
(2, 2) ▭
(2, 3) ▭
(3, 3) ▭
(3, 2) ▭
(1, 2) ▭

21
Pick n Mix ▭
Chocolate ▭
Toffees ▭
Lollies ▭
Gummy Bears ▭

22
A ▭
B ▭
C ▭
D ▭
E ▭

23
12.03 ▭
11.15 ▭
11.48 ▭
12.00 ▭
12.48 ▭

24
7.5 m ▭
7 m ▭
2.5 m ▭
5 m ▭
3 m ▭

25
10 minutes ▭
54 minutes ▭
4 minutes ▭
70 minutes ▭
64 minutes ▭

26
- 6 ☐
- 18 ☐
- 4 ☐
- 10 ☐
- 12 ☐

27
- 15 ☐
- 14 ☐
- 9 ☐
- 18 ☐
- 8 ☐

28
- 18 weeks ☐
- 12 weeks ☐
- 10 weeks ☐
- 15 weeks ☐
- 8 weeks ☐

29
- 12 ☐
- 20 ☐
- 6 ☐
- 24 ☐
- 18 ☐

30
- 18.5°C ☐
- 20.5°C ☐
- 18.3°C ☐
- 18.8°C ☐
- 16.5°C ☐

31
- 230 cm ☐
- 115 cm ☐
- 150 cm ☐
- 200 cm ☐
- 300 cm ☐

32
- 1980 ☐
- 1960 ☐
- 1950 ☐
- 2000 ☐
- 1800 ☐

33
- 0.003 ☐
- 0.3 ☐
- 0.03 ☐
- 3 ☐
- 30 ☐

34
- 18 children ☐
- 24 children ☐
- 52 children ☐
- 14 children ☐
- 42 children ☐

35
- A ☐
- B ☐
- C ☐
- D ☐
- E ☐

36
- 27 times ☐
- 9 times ☐
- 18 times ☐
- 2 times ☐
- 12 times ☐

37
- £15.50 ☐
- £375.00 ☐
- £250.00 ☐
- £25.00 ☐
- £37.50 ☐

38
- A ☐
- B ☐
- C ☐
- D ☐
- E ☐

39
- £40 ☐
- £60 ☐
- £120 ☐
- £80 ☐
- £50 ☐

40
- 1124 m ☐
- 3934 m ☐
- 3967 m ☐
- 3423 m ☐
- 1524 m ☐

41
- 108° ☐
- 82° ☐
- 90° ☐
- 72° ☐
- 180° ☐

42
- 5 ☐
- 50 ☐
- 10 ☐
- 100 ☐
- 60 ☐

43
- 16 cm ☐
- 6 cm ☐
- 10 cm ☐
- 9 cm ☐
- 3 cm ☐

44
- 10% ☐
- 0.1% ☐
- 1% ☐
- 0.01% ☐
- 100% ☐

45
- 100 mph ☐
- 60 mph ☐
- 70 mph ☐
- 40 mph ☐
- 50 mph ☐

46
- A ☐
- B ☐
- C ☐
- D ☐
- E ☐

47
- 10 ☐
- 24 ☐
- 6 ☐
- 12 ☐
- 15 ☐

48
- 64 minutes ☐
- 74 minutes ☐
- 84 minutes ☐
- 24 minutes ☐
- 36 minutes ☐

49
- 25 ☐
- 20 ☐
- 18 ☐
- 21 ☐
- 15 ☐

50
- A ☐
- B ☐
- C ☐
- D ☐
- E ☐

MATHS PRACTICE PAPER 2

Pupil's Name

School Name

Date of Test

PUPIL NUMBER

SCHOOL NUMBER

DATE OF BIRTH

Day	Month	Year
[0] [0]	January	2007
[1] [1]	February	2008
[2] [2]	March	2009
[3] [3]	April	2010
[4]	May	2011
[5]	June	2012
[6]	July	2013
[7]	August	2014
[8]	September	2015
[9]	October	2016
	November	2017
	December	2018

Please mark like this ⊢.

Pupil Number columns: [0]–[9] (six columns)
School Number columns: [0]–[9] (seven columns)

1
- 12.4
- 12.5
- 12.2
- 12.25
- 12.35

2
- 4.5°C
- 7.8°C
- 10.5°C
- 7.2°C
- 10.8°C

3
- 7095
- 7905
- 7950
- 70905
- 70950

4
- A
- B
- C
- D
- E

5
- Shape 1
- Shape 2
- Shape 3
- Shape 4
- Shape 5

6
- 50 minutes
- 47 minutes
- 43 minutes
- 45 minutes
- 48 minutes

7
- 13
- 8
- 10
- 20
- 5

8
- 8.45 am
- 8.15 am
- 8.05 am
- 9.30 am
- 9.45 am

9
- 1.5 litres
- 500 litres
- 15 litres
- 1500 litres
- 0.015 litres

10
- 180°
- 120°
- 60°
- 45°
- 90°

11
- −4
- 4
- 1
- −6
- 0

12
- Abby
- Bushra
- Chevelle
- Daria
- Emilia

13
- 4 litres
- 8 litres
- 10 litres
- 7 litres
- 5 litres

14
- 10
- 560
- 650
- 100
- 56

15
- 18 children
- 21 children
- 100 children
- 175 children
- 125 children

16
- 15
- 9
- 81
- 12
- 18

17
- A
- B
- C
- D
- E

18
- 3.00 pm
- 3.45 pm
- 5.00 pm
- 5.15 pm
- 2.00 pm

19
- 7
- 2
- 8
- 14
- 40

20
- 5890 km
- 6550 km
- 5920 km
- 6290 km
- 5620 km

21
- A
- B
- C
- D
- E

22
- Month 1
- Month 2
- Month 4
- Month 5
- Month 6

23
- £0.75
- £0.60
- £2.50
- £0.25
- £1.30

24
- A
- B
- C
- D
- E

25
- 35
- 28
- 7
- 14
- 10

26
- 21 cm ☐
- 2.1 cm ☐
- 21 m ☐
- 2.1 m ☐
- 210 mm ☐

27
- A ☐
- B ☐
- C ☐
- D ☐
- E ☐

28
- 48 cm ☐
- 24 cm ☐
- 12 cm ☐
- 10 cm ☐
- 6 cm ☐

29
- 10.8 m ☐
- 13.2 m ☐
- 7.0 m ☐
- 10.2 m ☐
- 7.8 m ☐

30
- 20 ☐
- 25 ☐
- 30 ☐
- 50 ☐
- 10 ☐

31
- (4, −7) ☐
- (−7, −4) ☐
- (7, 4) ☐
- (−4, −7) ☐
- (7, −4) ☐

32
- £44.90 ☐
- £52.30 ☐
- £47.90 ☐
- £45.30 ☐
- £32.90 ☐

33
- 9 ☐
- 15 ☐
- 13 ☐
- 16 ☐
- 12 ☐

34
- 30 sticks ☐
- 21 sticks ☐
- 25 sticks ☐
- 29 sticks ☐
- 35 sticks ☐

35
- A ☐
- B ☐
- C ☐
- D ☐
- E ☐

36
- 12 boxes ☐
- 10 boxes ☐
- 6 boxes ☐
- 8 boxes ☐
- 4 boxes ☐

37
- 300 times ☐
- 30 times ☐
- 100 times ☐
- 1000 times ☐
- 10 times ☐

38
- 150 children ☐
- 210 children ☐
- 300 children ☐
- 120 children ☐
- 100 children ☐

39
- (−3, −4) ☐
- (−3, 4) ☐
- (1, 4) ☐
- (4, 1) ☐
- (3, 4) ☐

40
- 18 cm ☐
- 28 cm ☐
- 36 cm ☐
- 30 cm ☐
- 15 cm ☐

41
- 62 edges ☐
- 60 edges ☐
- 120 edges ☐
- 122 edges ☐
- 110 edges ☐

42
- 87 minutes ☐
- 40 minutes ☐
- 52 minutes ☐
- 73 minutes ☐
- 67 minutes ☐

43
- A ☐
- B ☐
- C ☐
- D ☐
- E ☐

44
- A ☐
- B ☐
- C ☐
- D ☐
- E ☐

45
- 35° ☐
- 150° ☐
- 90° ☐
- 135° ☐
- 120° ☐

46
- 12 children ☐
- 24 children ☐
- 18 children ☐
- 16 children ☐
- 15 children ☐

47
- 1725 kg ☐
- 17.25 kg ☐
- 172.5 g ☐
- 1.725 kg ☐
- 17.25 g ☐

48
- Shape 1 ☐
- Shape 2 ☐
- Shape 3 ☐
- Shape 4 ☐
- Shape 5 ☐

49
- 300 people ☐
- 360 people ☐
- 180 people ☐
- 120 people ☐
- 240 people ☐

50
- 35 seconds ☐
- 40 seconds ☐
- 45 seconds ☐
- 41 seconds ☐
- 24 seconds ☐

Pupil's Name

School Name

Date of Test

PUPIL NUMBER

[0]	[0]	[0]	[0]	[0]	[0]
[1]	[1]	[1]	[1]	[1]	[1]
[2]	[2]	[2]	[2]	[2]	[2]
[3]	[3]	[3]	[3]	[3]	[3]
[4]	[4]	[4]	[4]	[4]	[4]
[5]	[5]	[5]	[5]	[5]	[5]
[6]	[6]	[6]	[6]	[6]	[6]
[7]	[7]	[7]	[7]	[7]	[7]
[8]	[8]	[8]	[8]	[8]	[8]
[9]	[9]	[9]	[9]	[9]	[9]

SCHOOL NUMBER

[0]	[0]	[0]	[0]	[0]	[0]	[0]
[1]	[1]	[1]	[1]	[1]	[1]	[1]
[2]	[2]	[2]	[2]	[2]	[2]	[2]
[3]	[3]	[3]	[3]	[3]	[3]	[3]
[4]	[4]	[4]	[4]	[4]	[4]	[4]
[5]	[5]	[5]	[5]	[5]	[5]	[5]
[6]	[6]	[6]	[6]	[6]	[6]	[6]
[7]	[7]	[7]	[7]	[7]	[7]	[7]
[8]	[8]	[8]	[8]	[8]	[8]	[8]
[9]	[9]	[9]	[9]	[9]	[9]	[9]

Please mark like this ⊢.

DATE OF BIRTH

Day		Month		Year	
[0]	[0]	January	▭	2007	▭
[1]	[1]	February	▭	2008	▭
[2]	[2]	March	▭	2009	▭
[3]	[3]	April	▭	2010	▭
	[4]	May	▭	2011	▭
	[5]	June	▭	2012	▭
	[6]	July	▭	2013	▭
	[7]	August	▭	2014	▭
	[8]	September	▭	2015	▭
	[9]	October	▭	2016	▭
		November	▭	2017	▭
		December	▭	2018	▭

1
- 200 513 ▭
- 20 530 ▭
- 25 013 ▭
- 2513 ▭
- 20 513 ▭

2
- 6 people ▭
- 12 people ▭
- 27 people ▭
- 9 people ▭
- 18 people ▭

3
- 732 cm ▭
- 733 cm ▭
- 73 cm ▭
- 73.3 cm ▭
- 73.2 cm ▭

4
- Obtuse ▭
- Acute ▭
- Reflex ▭
- Right angle ▭
- Straight angle ▭

5
- 25 kg ▭
- 2500 kg ▭
- 250 kg ▭
- 2.5 kg ▭
- 0.25 kg ▭

6
- Shape 1 ▭
- Shape 2 ▭
- Shape 3 ▭
- Shape 4 ▭
- Shape 5 ▭

7
- 38 640 ▭
- 9660 ▭
- 35 870 ▭
- 35 000 ▭
- 9770 ▭

8
- 9 minutes ▭
- 11 minutes ▭
- 12 minutes ▭
- 10 minutes ▭
- 8 minutes ▭

9
- 0.35 litres ▭
- 5 litres ▭
- 150 litres ▭
- 1.25 litres ▭
- 3.75 litres ▭

10
- 516 ▭
- 520 ▭
- 512 ▭
- 504 ▭
- 530 ▭

11
- A ▭
- B ▭
- C ▭
- D ▭
- E ▭

12
- 24 cm³ ▭
- 68 cm³ ▭
- 17 cm³ ▭
- 36 cm³ ▭
- 72 cm³ ▭

13
- 28 ▭
- 34 ▭
- 16 ▭
- 50 ▭
- 30 ▭

14
- 0.01 ▭
- 10 ▭
- 1000 ▭
- 0.1 ▭
- 100 ▭

15
- Gummy Bears ▭
- Lollies ▭
- Chocolates ▭
- Toffees ▭
- Other ▭

16
- (2, −4) ▭
- (2, 4) ▭
- (−2, 4) ▭
- (4, −2) ▭
- (4, 2) ▭

17
- A ▭
- B ▭
- C ▭
- D ▭
- E ▭

18
- 14.15 ▭
- 15.15 ▭
- 04.50 ▭
- 03.00 ▭
- 14.30 ▭

19
- 15 children ▭
- 30 children ▭
- 20 children ▭
- 25 children ▭
- 5 children ▭

20
- A ▭
- B ▭
- C ▭
- D ▭
- E ▭

21
- A ▭
- B ▭
- C ▭
- D ▭
- E ▭

22
- Road ▭
- School ▭
- Playground ▭
- Playing field ▭
- Trees ▭

23
- 48 minutes ▭
- 18 minutes ▭
- 26 minutes ▭
- 31 minutes ▭
- 50 minutes ▭

24
- 35 ▭
- 14 ▭
- 7 ▭
- 21 ▭
- 28 ▭

25
- 140° ▭
- 130° ▭
- 115° ▭
- 180° ▭
- 80° ▭

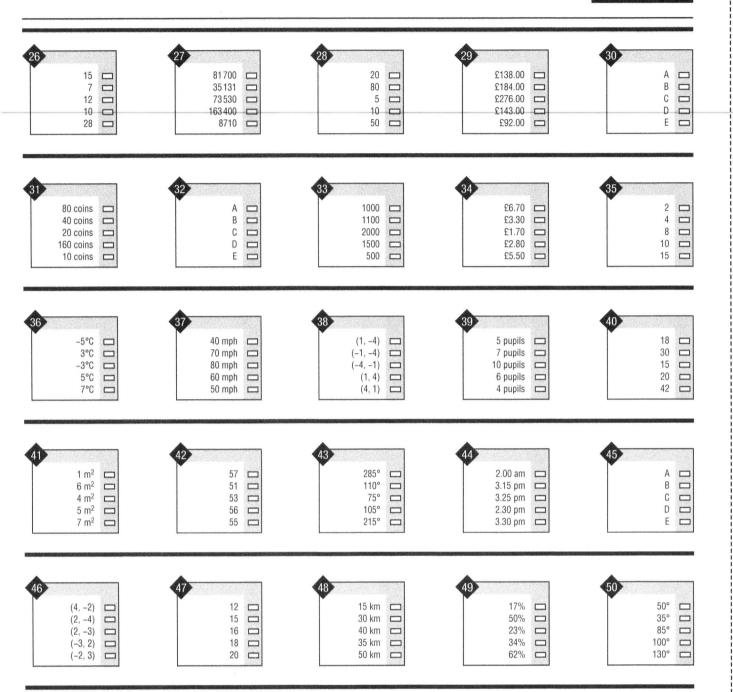

26
- 15
- 7
- 12
- 10
- 28

27
- 81 700
- 35 131
- 73 530
- 163 400
- 8710

28
- 20
- 80
- 5
- 10
- 50

29
- £138.00
- £184.00
- £276.00
- £143.00
- £92.00

30
- A
- B
- C
- D
- E

31
- 80 coins
- 40 coins
- 20 coins
- 160 coins
- 10 coins

32
- A
- B
- C
- D
- E

33
- 1000
- 1100
- 2000
- 1500
- 500

34
- £6.70
- £3.30
- £1.70
- £2.80
- £5.50

35
- 2
- 4
- 8
- 10
- 15

36
- −5°C
- 3°C
- −3°C
- 5°C
- 7°C

37
- 40 mph
- 70 mph
- 80 mph
- 60 mph
- 50 mph

38
- (1, −4)
- (−1, −4)
- (−4, −1)
- (1, 4)
- (4, 1)

39
- 5 pupils
- 7 pupils
- 10 pupils
- 6 pupils
- 4 pupils

40
- 18
- 30
- 15
- 20
- 42

41
- 1 m²
- 6 m²
- 4 m²
- 5 m²
- 7 m²

42
- 57
- 51
- 53
- 56
- 55

43
- 285°
- 110°
- 75°
- 105°
- 215°

44
- 2.00 am
- 3.15 pm
- 3.25 pm
- 2.30 pm
- 3.30 pm

45
- A
- B
- C
- D
- E

46
- (4, −2)
- (2, −4)
- (2, −3)
- (−3, 2)
- (−2, 3)

47
- 12
- 15
- 16
- 18
- 20

48
- 15 km
- 30 km
- 40 km
- 35 km
- 50 km

49
- 17%
- 50%
- 23%
- 34%
- 62%

50
- 50°
- 35°
- 85°
- 100°
- 130°

Pupil's Name

School Name

Date of Test

DATE OF BIRTH

Day	Month	Year
[0] [0]	January ☐	2007 ☐
[1] [1]	February ☐	2008 ☐
[2] [2]	March ☐	2009 ☐
[3] [3]	April ☐	2010 ☐
[4]	May ☐	2011 ☐
[5]	June ☐	2012 ☐
[6]	July ☐	2013 ☐
[7]	August ☐	2014 ☐
[8]	September ☐	2015 ☐
[9]	October ☐	2016 ☐
	November ☐	2017 ☐
	December ☐	2018 ☐

PUPIL NUMBER

| [0] [0] [0] [0] [0] [0] |
| [1] [1] [1] [1] [1] [1] |
| [2] [2] [2] [2] [2] [2] |
| [3] [3] [3] [3] [3] [3] |
| [4] [4] [4] [4] [4] [4] |
| [5] [5] [5] [5] [5] [5] |
| [6] [6] [6] [6] [6] [6] |
| [7] [7] [7] [7] [7] [7] |
| [8] [8] [8] [8] [8] [8] |
| [9] [9] [9] [9] [9] [9] |

SCHOOL NUMBER

| [0] [0] [0] [0] [0] [0] [0] |
| [1] [1] [1] [1] [1] [1] [1] |
| [2] [2] [2] [2] [2] [2] [2] |
| [3] [3] [3] [3] [3] [3] [3] |
| [4] [4] [4] [4] [4] [4] [4] |
| [5] [5] [5] [5] [5] [5] [5] |
| [6] [6] [6] [6] [6] [6] [6] |
| [7] [7] [7] [7] [7] [7] [7] |
| [8] [8] [8] [8] [8] [8] [8] |
| [9] [9] [9] [9] [9] [9] [9] |

Please mark like this ⊢.

1
- 2 tens ☐
- 2 hundreds ☐
- 2 thousands ☐
- 2 ones ☐
- 2 ten thousands ☐

2
- 18 children ☐
- 9 children ☐
- 15 children ☐
- 24 children ☐
- 12 children ☐

3
- 90° ☐
- 120° ☐
- 180° ☐
- 270° ☐
- 360° ☐

4
- 5p ☐
- 25p ☐
- 1p ☐
- 50p ☐
- 10p ☐

5
- 10 ☐
- 100 ☐
- 1000 ☐
- 0.1 ☐
- 0.01 ☐

6
- 105° ☐
- 75° ☐
- 180° ☐
- 360° ☐
- 45° ☐

7
- A ☐
- B ☐
- C ☐
- D ☐
- E ☐

8
- North ☐
- South-West ☐
- West ☐
- South-East ☐
- East ☐

9
- A ☐
- B ☐
- C ☐
- D ☐
- E ☐

10
- Rectangle ☐
- Trapezium ☐
- Rhombus ☐
- Hexagon ☐
- Triangle ☐

11
- 15 ☐
- 30 ☐
- 40 ☐
- 13 ☐
- 8 ☐

12
- A ☐
- B ☐
- C ☐
- D ☐
- E ☐

13
- A ☐
- B ☐
- C ☐
- D ☐
- E ☐

14
- A ☐
- B ☐
- C ☐
- D ☐
- E ☐

15
- 100 ☐
- 75 ☐
- 175 ☐
- 200 ☐
- 50 ☐

16
- 7 ☐
- 21 ☐
- 14 ☐
- 12 ☐
- 25 ☐

17
- 57 minutes ☐
- 74 minutes ☐
- 43 minutes ☐
- 1 hour 30 minutes ☐
- 32 minutes ☐

18
- 100 books ☐
- 55 books ☐
- 45 books ☐
- 75 books ☐
- 60 books ☐

19
- 12 ☐
- 6 ☐
- 21 ☐
- 15 ☐
- 18 ☐

20
- 10 ☐
- 8 ☐
- 12 ☐
- 14 ☐
- 16 ☐

21
- 35 760 ☐
- 86 400 ☐
- 32 400 ☐
- 36 000 ☐
- 91 300 ☐

22
- 30 ☐
- 12 ☐
- 90 ☐
- 42 ☐
- 126 ☐

23
- (−13, −4) ☐
- (−8, −4) ☐
- (1, −4) ☐
- (1, 2) ☐
- (−8, 2) ☐

24
- 250 g ☐
- 275 g ☐
- 375 g ☐
- 320 g ☐
- 500 g ☐

25
- A ☐
- B ☐
- C ☐
- D ☐
- E ☐

26
A ☐
B ☐
C ☐
D ☐
E ☐

27
75 ☐
90 ☐
60 ☐
15 ☐
10 ☐

28
A ☐
B ☐
C ☐
D ☐
E ☐

29
64 ☐
60 ☐
61 ☐
63 ☐
62 ☐

30
7 ☐
8 ☐
10 ☐
6 ☐
9 ☐

31
1600 cm^2 ☐
128 m^2 ☐
160 cm^2 ☐
12.8 m^2 ☐
1280 cm^2 ☐

32
15 m^3 ☐
130 m^3 ☐
60 m^3 ☐
0.06 m^3 ☐
0.15 m^3 ☐

33
7 ☐
19 ☐
9 ☐
14 ☐
12 ☐

34
73.068 ☐
73.662 ☐
73.062 ☐
73.122 ☐
73.014 ☐

35
A ☐
B ☐
C ☐
D ☐
E ☐

36
10 months ☐
4 months ☐
3 months ☐
5 months ☐
8 months ☐

37
60° ☐
120° ☐
270° ☐
240° ☐
315° ☐

38
£100 ☐
£35 ☐
£150 ☐
£70 ☐
£200 ☐

39
12 minutes ☐
15 minutes ☐
75 minutes ☐
31 minutes ☐
42 minutes ☐

40
A ☐
B ☐
C ☐
D ☐
E ☐

41
20 ☐
16 ☐
40 ☐
8 ☐
32 ☐

42
8 cm ☐
30 cm ☐
95 cm ☐
26 cm ☐
10 cm ☐

43
£42 ☐
£54 ☐
£84 ☐
£90 ☐
£108 ☐

44
A ☐
B ☐
C ☐
D ☐
E ☐

45
40 mph ☐
30 mph ☐
10 mph ☐
50 mph ☐
70 mph ☐

46
200 ml ☐
1500 ml ☐
400 ml ☐
800 ml ☐
1600 ml ☐

47
7 ☐
12 ☐
10 ☐
8 ☐
5 ☐

48
45° ☐
30° ☐
50° ☐
90° ☐
100° ☐

49
21 ☐
24 ☐
18 ☐
20 ☐
25 ☐

50
Isosceles triangle ☐
Trapezium ☐
Rectangle ☐
Scalene triangle ☐
Kite ☐